A WALK IN THE COOL OF THE DAY

by

David E. Wright

A WALK IN THE COOL OF THE DAY

Copyright ©2025 David E. Wright

Copyright ©2025 David E. Wright, Livingston, Tennessee. All rights reserved. This book or any portion thereof may not be reproduced or used whatsoever without the express written consent of the publisher excepting the use of brief quotations in a book review or scholarly journal.

Cover photograph Copyright ©2025 by David E. Wright, Livingston, Tennessee. All rights reserved.

All scriptures taken from The Holy Bible, King James Version

In Memory of my Son

Alexander David Martin Wright

February 15, 1993 – April 6, 2011

TABLE OF CONTENTS

	Acknowledgements	7
	Introduction	9
1	Storm Warnings	12
2	Alone	21
3	Give Us Barabbas	32
4	An Angel Before Thee	40
5	Who Did It	49
6	Figuring Out the Bad Things	58
7	With All My Heart	68
8	Images	77
9	Thinking Jesus Through	89
10	Heart, Soul and…….Mind	98
11	Old Shirts	108
12	The Woman and the Broken Flask	119
13	Checking the Boxes	129
14	The Total You	138
15	A Walk in the Cool of the Day	146
	About the Author	156

Acknowledgements

My wife, Denise, for all the care and love she has selflessly given me for forty five years. A registered nurse, a very good one at that, Denise is largely responsible for my continuing survival and relative physical stability during this eighteen year battle with Wegener's Granulomatosis and the loss of our son.

Scott McKinney, my pastor, has tasked me continuously to deepen my faith as he delivers God's message to his congregation. He is as gifted a speaker as I have ever heard and his sermons and counsel are those I make mention of in this work. From the pulpit he challenged me to do what God was asking me to do that I had been avoiding. He does that. He challenges one to act. Maybe a question we should all answer, "What has God called you to do that you haven't done?"

Horace Burks, a former employer of mine and very close personal friend. We discussed heaven to many controversial conclusions. A gifted speaker and student of scripture in his own right, Horace provided much guidance in scripture interpretation and understanding throughout my adult life. He was there for me through illness and loss more than just a few times.

Introduction

*"Jesus said unto him, Thou shalt love the Lord
thy God with all thy heart,
and with all thy soul, and with all thy mind."
Matthew 22:37 KJV*

Out of the blackness, from the darkness into the light is a transition from total self reliance to walking in victory with God, a walk in the cool of the day so to speak. This writer shares his journey herein from the total self to the growing need for and reliance on a loving, saving connection with God, a real and deeply personal relationship. Salvation is critically important but salvation alone just assures one entry into heaven at death. Walking with God is a lifelong pursuit once on the path.

But I assert that there is so much more than salvation to a relationship with the Creator of all that is and ever will be. For so many years, decades long in fact, I was safe in the eternal arms of Jesus and I still am. And though nothing was missing from the salvation afforded me by grace through faith I felt I was leaving a lot on the spiritual table. I was walking alone. I was ignoring the counsel promised to me. And sure, I prayed just as often as I needed something.

 I always said I believed everything in the Bible years before actually reading the Bible. Having read the Bible, from the first verse of Genesis to the last verse of Revelation several times I can still say I believe it all. But this time is different. I know what it says, all of it. I haven't committed the entirety of scripture to memory. And I don't understand it all. And so I read and study and then read some more. If I don't understand what I'm reading I read it again. I pray on it. I ask questions of those more knowledgeable than I am and I prove out with scripture what I am told from the pulpit or otherwise. Most of all, I ask God to give me understanding.

I finally arrived at one certain conclusion. I don't know everything nor will I ever. But I know the One who does and He is available to me all the time. He's never too busy to speak to my heart, reason with my mind and enrich my soul. I just had to stop being so self reliant and self confident and place my trust, all of my trust, in God. That was very hard for me to do even after being saved. I fully believe that God gave us certain abilities to use in our pursuit of happiness. But I learned the hard way that there is no happiness walking alone.

I learned that God does use all things for the good of those who love Him. That's hard to see sometimes. And I describe some of these times in the chapters that follow. God's plan for each of us is not always transparent, not always instantly understood. Often it is unveiled over months or years as were several instances in my life. But it is always for our good. That good might be found in an early arrival into heaven or an exceptionally long life. But whatever God's plan is for me I want to abide in that plan.

My walk with God is a bit unconventional as compared to today's churchgoing Christian. And you will understand why in these pages as I present to you my evolving walk with God. And though God doesn't come here in the flesh in the cool of the day anymore, I would strongly assert that walk with Him is still available. It was hard for me to recognize the opportunity to walk more closely with Him as I kept relying on myself and my abilities to succeed in life. The harder I tried the more difficult and distant spiritual fidelity seemed.

But through continual study, fasting, serious prayer just as Jesus taught, and listening to God I believe I have been able to resume that walk with God in the cool of the day. The spiritual ears don't require much training, just being willing to listen and eager to hear what God has to say to each of us. No, the Almighty doesn't join me in the flesh, but that walk with Him is still available. The words I have recorded herein tell of my journey out of the blackness of my own world into a walk in His world, the world of eternity.......of heaven.

Let's walk........

Chapter 1

Storm Warnings

As I write, we have had storm warnings every day or two. Either a severe thunderstorm watch or a flash flood watch or both have been in place during large parts of the day. Less frequently, but a little more serious, are the actual thunderstorm warnings that come our way. And even less frequently the dreaded tornado warning comes blaring through the weather radio that normally sits silently on the chest of drawers in the bedroom. Flash flood warnings, straight line winds, thunder and lightning usually accompany these warnings. Here in middle Tennessee we get them all in nearly every season. We even had a blizzard warning a few years ago and the blizzard actually showed up. Tennessee is no stranger to snow storms, ice storms and occasional temperatures below zero and above one hundred. I don't think we have had a hurricane warning though some hurricanes survived far enough inland to bring on a tropical storm warning.

We get all kinds of warnings and all kinds of weather here. Tennessee is known for presenting all types of weather in and out of season, in fact, sometimes during the same day. With these warnings come the investigations that follow. These investigations ensue immediately upon being warned. Some of us gaze at the radar to see if we are in the path of a storm. We watch the weather probably more than we watch the national news. A protest in Washington or New York just doesn't affect us as directly as does a five inch rain or an F2 tornado in the front yard, or worse, in the living room. My family has felt the direct effects of a tornado up close and personal, just the thickness of a concrete block away.

I have been in a tornado before with lightning strikes so close I could hear the ominous click of the lightning bolt finding its way to ground. I can still remember the super tornado outbreak in 1974. I was in high school at the time and a cousin and I were "riding around" in town. Night had fallen but the lightning was nearly continuous. It was beautiful and scary at the same time. We knew something big was going on but had no idea people were dying in this storm just in walking distance of our homes. I don't know if there were warnings issued or not. Very likely we were listening to a cassette tape or a popular Chicago radio station while it was all occurring. As the night wore on the sound of sirens from emergency vehicles filled what was normally relative silence on the Cumberland Plateau. And they continued well into the next day.

The next morning, as sunrise displayed the damage, the sky took on a gray tone reflecting the loss of life in our town. We knew these people, those killed by the storm. Homes were removed from where they sat. In some cases, the tornado left no evidence that a home was ever there. In other cases, insulation and sheet metal littered the grounds of homes that appeared to have exploded. Cows and horses were killed by flying debris and lightning strikes, thousands and thousands of trees were laid waste and farm fences were down all over. On our small farm were over 300 large, fully mature, oak, hickory and ash trees uprooted and twisted, treetops snapped off like twigs. You would just have to have seen it to believe it. Our Black Angus bull was struck by lightning and stood dead on all four legs. My parents were vacationing in Greece and returned to what appeared to be a war zone.

We were not alone. As a matter of fact, our family and farm got the light end of the storm. Devastation was less than a mile away. We had significant damage to timber but suffered no personal injury. The barn and chicken house had extensive damage. Other areas of the country were also hit with tornados. It seemed the wrath of God had manifested itself in this weather. The damage all up and down the middle part of the United States resulted in a large parts of the country being declared disaster areas. Our reaction to weather warnings had been taken rather nonchalantly in the past but this event changed that in an instant. Warnings seemed to be issued more frequently and received with urgency unlike any reaction before. Later I learned from my parents that devastating storms seem to repeat on an unpredictable frequency separated sometimes by fifty or sixty years, sometimes longer. They didn't view these storms as once and never again occurrences. Death and destruction comes calling.

To the basement, yes, the basement is where we go now during a threatening storm. Our home seems to be quite secure and we are thankful for that. Cell phone in one hand and a blanket or pillow in the other, we head down the steps to the relative security of the basement. If you can hear the storm from our basement it is truly a bad storm. The most ominous sound is that of a train or whine of a large turbine engine just outside followed by debris falling on whatever remains above you. We are probably more prepared than most. We have a secure home though still no match for a large tornado. We have a generator in the event we lose electricity, a cache of bottled water and a few items of food in case we are unable to get to town. And we have each other, at least presently. We enjoy a sense of security that seems certain. It is not. The elements can present enough power to totally destroy our home and end our lives in the process and it can do it in just a minute or two.

We take warnings seriously, especially the dreaded tornado warning. Speaking for both my wife and myself I can say that neither of us fears death. We just think it wise to avoid injury and pain whenever we can, especially when it's no more difficult than changing our location in our home. Others take weather warnings completely in stride, never acting to take advantage of whatever protection is available. I'm not sure whether that's brave or foolish. I suppose it can be both, either or neither depending on the circumstances. And I try not to be critical of the choices of others so long as their choices don't place others in danger. A storm can be no more than a threat, an injurious and crippling event or it can be the end of your life on earth. So heed the warnings as you will. We have them, we know what they mean, and we mostly know what to do during the warning period. These warnings usually precede the possible event by a few minutes or sometimes even hours unlike other types of warnings we have been given.

Some warnings are in print for us. They remain in effect. We largely ignore them as have our ancestors through time. In fact, the earliest recorded warning came from God warning Adam not to eat of the fruit of the tree of knowledge in the Garden of Eden. People ignore this warning as did Adam and Eve. The consequences were not exactly extraordinary though eternally far reaching. The consequences were known to Adam before they flaunted the warning and disobeyed. Death came to earth. The earth suffered a curse in which we find ourselves continuing in today. Unlike the relative safety of our basement in a storm, there is no manmade safe place from the judgment of God.

"And the LORD God commanded the man, saying, Of every tree of the garden thou mayest freely eat: But of the tree of the knowledge of good and evil, thou shalt not eat of it: for in the day that thou eatest thereof thou shalt surely die." Genesis 2:16-17 KJV

We just don't seem to be able to control ourselves in the face of temptation. And we seem to be a quite gullible species though made in the image of God. One must wonder why Eve's choice was what it was in the face of the facts. Maybe she didn't know that God spoke the entirety of creation into being. Could she have been out of the loop when God walked with them during the cool of the day? Had she no knowledge that God made her? Eve wasn't born. She was made by God Himself from material taken from Adam, a rib. Maybe her life experience had little exposure to being misled. Whatever the reason, she and Adam both knew what the rule was and disobeyed the Creator and Maker having been warned of the consequences. Their relationship with God was over. It was dead. And they, too, would die. The world endures even today the curse brought by disobedience. I just have to wonder why God didn't just call the whole thing off right there. I believe it was and is just as He said. He loved the world. It was His creation, His work. And He was not surprised by any of it. He warned Adam and Eve of the consequences of disobedience and they chose unwisely. We do it all the time. I think sometimes we look down on Eve for her decision when in reality we would have all probably succumbed to the temptation.

Looking back, I wonder how much of my motivation to accept Christ's payment for my sins was motivated by God's original warning. Was I afraid of dying? Of course, that weighed heavily on the mind of a nine year old having first been exposed to the reality of death. Peer pressure also played a part I suppose. Our Cub Scout den mother had passed away recently and I really loved her. Her passing struck hard on this boy. So death became so real to me. I had lost pets to passing cars on the highway and to the pets' old age before. The death of a pet was to be expected. I knew from the earliest age that my pets were temporary companions, very temporary indeed. But the loss of my den mother was quite different. There was the mutual exchange of love between human beings that cannot be replicated with the relationship with an animal.

So I was not concerned for my life at the time. I was young and had not been exposed to childhood death yet. But I had been exposed to my part of sin and the association sin has with death, spiritual or otherwise. I had guilt. I was guilty and I knew it. Conviction had set in and it was overwhelming. Naturally enough for me, I had aisle dread. Though I grew out of it as an adult I was quite bashful as a child. I dreaded walking that aisle at church in front of everyone. I was not ashamed of my decision and my decision was sound. Walk it I did. And I was baptized a few days later. Guilt was lifted and relief was afforded. I knew someday death would fall on me but not the death Adam and Eve were warned of.

Through the years I think on it a lot, salvation that is. Why is something so fundamental so hard to really embrace. I've heard it all I think. The decision many make is simply a mechanical acknowledgement of their desire to avoid hell. Nowhere I'm familiar with in the Bible mentions walking an aisle, shaking the preacher's hand and standing in a receiving line while church members pass by with congratulations and handshakes. Nowhere in the Bible do I recall a passage where if one wants to avoid hell, all one must do is to go through the motions with meaningless affirmative nods when asked the critical questions. That's the difference in being born again and faking salvation. Avoiding hell is not a decision, it's a consequence. Heaven is the same thing. It is a consequence of repenting one's sins, believing in and accepting Jesus' payment for one's sins. We have been warned.

"For God so loved the world, that He gave his only begotten Son, that whosoever believeth in Him should not perish, but have everlasting life. For God sent not his Son into the world to condemn the world; but that the world through Him might be saved. He that believeth on Him is not condemned: but he that believeth not is condemned already, because he hath not believed in the name of the only begotten Son of God."
John 3:16-18 KJV

Preachers are the weathermen of life, everlasting life. They carry God's warning to us frequently. The pastor I knew the best was criticized for always including the plan of salvation anytime and anywhere he preached. Though it was not in his "job description" it was in his calling. That I know of, even at funerals and in weddings, he always managed to present the plan of salvation. I was amused at the criticism leveled at him. There can be no more important message from the pulpit than the warning of the eternal storm, everlasting separation from God, death though cursed with an inability to die.

I have acted on the warning. I have the security only afforded by a penitent admission and active acknowledgment that Christ paid for my sins and is the very Son of God. So why do I still listen to the preacher? It's the relationship thing you know. Salvation is the reservation section of eternal life, the starting point for a vibrant, growing, one on One relationship with the Creator of all that is. I still listen to purely evangelical, plan of salvation sermons but I find much to be learned in preaching from the whole of the Bible. The anointed messenger of God has the ability to call the listener to action given ears tuned in to what God has to say.

"Submit yourselves therefore to God. Resist the devil, and he will flee from you." James 2:8 KJV

"But grow in grace, and *in* the knowledge of our Lord and Saviour Jesus Christ. To him *be* glory both now and for ever. Amen." II Peter 3:18 KJV

So there's not just the warning of death for the commission of sin. The Bible is full of warnings. Some of these warnings are implicit in that they show certain consequences for certain acts. Moses wasn't allowed entry into the Promised Land because of disobedience. Indeed, he could see the Promised Land but was not allowed to enter. To you and me, the penalty might seem excessive but it's still the penalty. Moses died in sight of the Promised Land. Earlier in history God destroyed mankind by flood and we are warned even now that the future destruction of the earth will be by heat. It's far off, right? So we believe.

"The Lord is not slack concerning his promise, as some men count slackness; but is longsuffering to us-ward, not willing

that any should perish, but that all should come to repentance. But the day of the Lord will come as a thief in the night; in the which the heavens shall pass away with a great noise, and the elements shall melt with fervent heat, the earth also and the works that are therein shall be burned up." II Peter 3:9-10 KJV

Moses delivered many warnings from God to pharaoh of plagues if he failed to let God's people go free. These warnings were of imminent Divine action. They were timed very close between the warning and the penalty. And the warning of death seems so distant in comparison. And it is distant, timed to end precisely at our physical death. We have all the time we have remaining in life to react to this warning. It would have been so convenient had God made it a date definite but then God seems to give us the entirety of our lives to heed this warning.

And it seems a bit disjointed doesn't it. The penalty, the wages of sin is death. But the payment for our sin is the affirmative, penitent belief in Christ, as the Son of God, paying for our sins. So why didn't God give the warning thusly: If you fail to acknowledge Christ as your Savior, you will face eternal torment? It's because there's more to salvation than just belief, but it's not anything you or I can do. Back to God's warning, something had to die, the offender had to die. I had to die!

My death wouldn't pay my debt. I am flawed. Sacrifice for my sin had to come from a like kind, one without blemish, clothed in total innocence. And that's why Jesus is truly the only suitable sacrifice for my sins. Had Jesus sinned, even the least infraction, He would have been an insufficient sacrifice for my sins. He would have been blemished and therefore not perfect for a once and done atonement. So He came. He lived. He walked the earth. He performed many miracles. He cured the sick and delivered the possessed from demons. He surrendered

Himself to a judgment for my sins. And He gave His life for me. He redeemed me.

So the warning of the outcome for sin was ignored by me too. I am as guilty as anyone ever was. And I didn't sign up to go to heaven. I haven't had my name removed from the rolls of hell. I could do neither. But Jesus has written my name down in the Lamb's Book of Life. And it's not because of any physical act I performed. No! It is because Jesus did. He did all the work for my salvation. He paid for it! All that was required of me was to realize my hopelessness and receive Him as my Savior. And the storm warning is lifted.

"But God, who is rich in mercy, for his great love wherewith he loved us, Even when we were dead in sins, hath quickened us together with Christ, (by grace ye are saved;) And hath raised us up together, and made us sit together in heavenly places in Christ Jesus: That in the ages to come he might shew the exceeding riches of his grace in his kindness toward us through Christ Jesus. For by grace are ye saved through faith; and that not of yourselves: it is the gift of God: Not of works, lest any man should boast. For we are his workmanship, created in Christ Jesus unto good works, which God hath before ordained that we should walk in them. Amen." Ephesians 2:4-10 KJV

Heaven and hell are consequences, they are destinations. They are not nor ever have they been decisions. You can't ask for one or the other. You can't make a reservation. You cannot work your way to salvation. Only Jesus can do that. And He did it too. He did it for me and you. Are you still under the promise of destruction?

Why?

Chapter 2

Alone

"A Psalm of David. The LORD *is* my shepherd; I shall not want. He maketh me to lie down in green pastures: he leadeth me beside the still waters.   He restoreth my soul: he leadeth me in the paths of righteousness for his name's sake.   Yea, though I walk through the valley of the shadow of death, I will fear no evil: for thou *art* with me; thy rod and thy staff they comfort me.   Thou preparest a table before me in the presence of mine enemies: thou anointest my head with oil; my cup runneth over.   Surely goodness and mercy shall follow me all the days of my life: and I will dwell in the house of the LORD for ever." Psalms 23 KJV

Being alone, feeling as if I'm alone, can sometimes be very troubling. More often than not, I really appreciate being alone. It's not that I don't enjoy being in the company of family and friends. Indeed, I do like company! But when I am in need of carefully considering things, things like the options available to me in making a decision or determining my stand on an issue, being alone is more often than not an advantage. But are we ever truly, genuinely alone?

I'm convinced that I am never truly alone. Someone or something is always around watching or listening. I might be without human company but in my environment, very often outside, I'm never alone. There is always a squirrel, bird, lizard, ant or countless other creatures nearby, near enough to both see and hear me if I make a noise or even move. Quite likely they don't care what I am doing as long as I don't pose a threat to them. Likewise, I don't care much about them either unless they pose a threat to me as in the instances of a hornet or a cornered squirrel. I consider that being truly alone but not genuinely alone.

I define being genuinely alone as being alone in the absolute, alone without other creatures nearby or aware of my presence, alone without any reminder that anything else is in close proximity to me that might be aware of my presence. That is really hard to achieve, genuinely being alone. It's becoming less difficult lately. As I write just now I am outside on the patio sitting under an umbrella on a hard aluminum chair. I am reminded that I am not genuinely alone by the bug bites and those bipeds using the highway in front of my house tuning their vehicles for maximum exhaust volume. Some of them start reminding me as far as five miles away. Sound carries in the Tennessee hills and hollows. The birds are singing and the trees move in the wind, dampening the intrusion of manmade noise.

There is a mechanical device in the pool cleaning the bottom and sides. It doesn't remind me that I am not genuinely alone. As far as I can tell it neither hears nor sees. It does its job starting in one end of the pool, occasionally surfacing for whatever reason, but it doesn't remind me of anything to do with being alone. To the contrary, it's actually an extension of my being alone doing my work, cleaning the pool after last night's electrical storm while receiving a bonus of torrential rain. This robotic device even assists my effort when I truly want to be alone by affording me the time so to be. So I am about as alone as most other times right now. The birds aren't disturbing my thoughts, the citronella lantern sitting at my feet has kept the biting bugs held off for the time being and the highway noise is just mindlessly interrupting like it always is. The pool robot is doing its thing and I'm trying to write about being alone, about why there is no such thing. And I've been close to being alone a few times. Those times made me realize the value of being alone with a single Entity presenting to me the knowledge that I'm never alone.

For more than twenty years we lived in a house on a mountain top within the city limits of our chosen hometown. I loved it there because it was convenient to the town but quite private. Feeling alone was easy though it was my first realization that being alone is a choice of perspective, not an actual thing. It was summer and I was thinning out a thicket in a fence row. It was overgrown with multiple hazards like poison ivy, wild blackberries and other briars whose mention fails to serve any purpose for my argument. The weather was hot and sticky that day. I don't know what the humidity or temperature was that day, but I know it was hot. I had an unhealthy habit of not drinking enough water when I was younger. With kidney disease, now in my mid-sixties, it's essential. But back then I only drank water when I just felt I had to. This time I felt I had to but I didn't have the energy to go get it.

The sweat had stopped keeping me cool. In fact, I had stopped sweating altogether. Though still very hot my body had stopped sweating. I suppose I should have known that to be a warning sign. So I sat down under a wild cherry tree to cool off. Even though it was the middle of summer and everything was so colorfully in bloom, I lost the sense of color in my vision. I remember it quite well. As everything turned from living color to black and white my heart calmed to a slow rate, my breathing slowed down and I was the calmest I could ever remember being. I felt I could have sat there under that tree forever. I thought I was alone. As it turned out my wife noticed the lack of activity and brought out water. A few drinks of water and my vision returned to normal and I was again able to sweat. But during that departure from normal function what I felt was almost like a different reality. I felt calm, resolute, and ready for whatever might be next no matter what or where it was. I was not alone in my thought. I was ready and willing to sit there from that moment on. Heat stroke? Dehydration? Both? Maybe it was just heightened focus of the unseen world.

On another occasion my father and I were hunting in what now is the Big South Fork National River and Recreation Area. As we traveled to the remote spot just a little east and north of Hatfield Ridge near the border with Kentucky, we saw no evidence of another human being. It was a seven and a half mile four wheel drive trek through the woods. We decided to split up to cover more area. It was brutally cold and frozen, crunchy snow was on the ground. I was about a hundred yards north of the Terry Cemetery road and east of a road, really a trail, that I think was referred to as the Boy Jordan road. It's been a long time so my incomplete recollection of road and trail names in a place as remote as I was in should be forgivable. I remember there was abundant sign of wild pigs nearby. The snow was glazed over and though I felt I was alone, with each step I loudly announced my presence to anything else in hearing of my steps, assuring it that it was not alone either.

I sat on the ground against a big tree. I don't remember the species. I just know it was the tail end of the hunting season and very cold and everything was frozen motionless. I was so alone. There was not any kind of movement, not so much as a breath of wind. The moisture in my breath froze almost immediately upon being exhaled. My boots were not suitable for cold and damp weather hunting by today's standards so my feet got cold first. It was almost like my experience with being too hot though that happened later in my life. I can say they were similar now that they both are past events. I didn't know what was happening to me but I knew something was. The colder I got the more acutely black and white everything became. Most everything was already black and white just because it was winter and snow was on everything. The setting of the sun was imminent. But this black and white was eerie.

As I became less sensitive to the cold my vision blurred and I really wanted to take a nap. Some common sense still prevailed and I decided I needed to try to stay awake until time to meet up at the vehicle to go home. I was alone. There was absolutely no movement in the woods, not even a puff of wind. The small game animals didn't stir, nothing moved. Even the clouds in the white background sky seemed glued in place. I went from freezing to being very satisfied with my place and condition at that moment. Was it just my physical condition or was I threatened by the cold? I cannot remember the temperature that day but I do remember the high was in the low teens. I felt it. Though very cold I was happy where I was. As far as satisfaction goes I believe I could've sat there quite pleased for the rest of my life. I sensed being alone, isolated. But I sensed the same presence that later in life would accompany me under the stress of the heat or dehydration. It was a state of pleasurable existence, a gravely pleasurable mortal threat. Or, maybe it was only and simply life-threatening. Whatever it was I felt I was truly alone but genuinely in company for sure.

Nobody reached out to me this time. Dad hadn't a clue of my precise location and one could wander around in that wilderness for weeks without finding the remains of another. But as black and white started turning mostly black I got up and started toward the vehicle. It felt more like a mechanical operation than a cognizant decision, as if I was programmed to do the right thing. I didn't have much to say on the trip home until I warmed up. After everything turned black and white I didn't notice the cold. I didn't notice much of anything. But, the presence, the feeling that I was not alone was overwhelmingly comforting. It all seemed as it should be. It seemed right. Once I returned to "normal" I missed the company I kept while I was truly alone yet not genuinely alone.

While under treatment for several diseases in my life I have taken some strong medications. Never has this type of a presence been sensed by me as a result of medication. It would seem nothing would replicate this presence. No I.V. bag, no syringe and no pill would replicate this sense of an overwhelming presence. It was not until my son was killed in a car crash that I became convinced that I knew what it was. I found the state of being alone, even isolation, and even in the presence of others. It didn't matter where I was or who was with me that I knew this Presence was clearly with me all the time. I just hadn't paid it much attention until those times that it was all that was left for me to notice. I sought it out. I knew it was real though I couldn't see it or touch it, an unseen Presence. But I knew I needed it. I needed it with me. I needed what it had for me.

It kind of took over for a time. It made no sound but it guided me. It led me to answers to questions. It assured me of personal worth and purpose at a time I could not possibly have cared less about living another day. I realized as I discovered Who it was that it had always been with me, always been available, always been willing to counsel and provide guidance and always capable of chastising me when I was guilty. The more I knew the Presence was real, was always with me, the more I concentrated on listening to what its discernibly inaudible voice had to say. The more I listened the more it seemed to have for me to hear. It became more active in my everyday life.

I liken it to my conscience although I believe the conscience has multiple, well, at least two faces. Unlike the cartoon, devil on one shoulder and angel on the other, I don't believe they communicate with each other. No, I believe the Holy Spirit is definitely one of the faces and the other is the demonic influence whether a demon or even Satan himself. Recognizing the voice of the faces is vital in deciding how to handle one's life. One will make everything bad, everything destructive, and everything sinful and appear so appealing as to be almost beyond our ability to resist. The other, the voice of the Holy

Spirit, will provide counsel and direction even though we find it often so convenient to resist.

I am convinced that during my two episodes, one of heat and one of cold, that I might have been physically affected but I never felt that I was alone. Indeed, I was in the safest and most pleasant company available. The Third person of God was with me. He always had been with me but in those two threatening circumstances He was the only one left. I will always believe that is why it was so comforting in both circumstances of physical distress. The focus on Him, even when I didn't realize it was Him, just has the effect of being in the presence of Divinity that nothing else can replicate. It is unmistakable.

For many years now I haven't had to reproduce the black and white separation from the world to sense His presence. I sense it all the time. I can literally be genuinely alone with Him while being truly in a crowd. Once I realized Who it was and how real He is, and knowing how to tune in, I can draw my focus to Him anywhere, anytime. The more focused on Him I become the more pleasant life is. And even with the loss of my son I know I'm never alone. And what good is His presence if one never listens to Him.

I think recognizing Him, His presence, is what makes me appreciate hunting and fishing more than ever. I really don't care about ever shooting another living thing. But I appreciate His handiwork most when I am alone in His spectacular creation. I really haven't scratched the surface of all those things He spoke into being but I'm looking. It's easy to listen for Him and to Him in the early morning hours of a beautiful sunrise or the fury of a thunderstorm. The majesty of a hundred year old oak tree or the decaying trunk of a tulip poplar tree converted to bird condominiums by pileated woodpeckers. Channels cut through limestone by the benign force of flowing water and the gaze of extreme distance into the heavens of infinity. All of these testify to His immensity and power. And I sense them all much better when it is just me and Him.

"For the invisible things of Him from the creation of the world are clearly seen, being understood by the things that are made, even His eternal power and Godhead: so that they are without excuse" Romans 1:20 KJV

He is good for peace. He is good for understanding. He is good for direction and counsel. He is good for patient longing. Healing, He is good for that. He is good for a check on our actions both good and bad. He is good for love when we are loveless. He is good for forgiveness when we are without excuse. He is good for everlasting life when death is what we deserve. He is good forever and for everything.

Have you sensed His presence? It is a not-so-hard cognizance that we all are capable of. It is essential to living the life that God has for us to live. We are incapable of a life pleasing to God without Him in our lives. Though I would rather have him here with me, I consider myself blessed that my son has already gone on before me. He has seen the face of God. He is in His presence as I write. He is eternally secure. And I believe this blessing stems from the fact that my only son died too. For sure, the circumstances were very different but the loss is still felt. And just as sure as I am that Jesus sits at the right hand of the Father, I am sure that my son is there, safe, home, living his everlasting life, hearing his discernibly audible voice. And God's only Son was the provision for the everlasting life of my son.

Alone, are we? Are we ever? Of course we are not. He is always with us. Contentment, indeed life, can be best with that Presence active, fully voiced and solitarily alone with us in all that we do. And everlasting life is only available through Christ Jesus. It is eternally critical that we cultivate that time alone, alone with God. And one day that Presence will be face to Face. I so look forward to that day.

"There is therefore now no condemnation to them which are in Christ Jesus, who walk not after the flesh, but after the Spirit. For the law of the Spirit of life in Christ Jesus hath made me free from the law of sin and death. For what the law could not do, in that it was weak through the flesh, God sending his own Son in the likeness of sinful flesh, and for sin, condemned sin in the flesh: That the righteousness of the law might be fulfilled in us, who walk not after the flesh, but after the Spirit. For they that are after the flesh do mind the things of the flesh; but they that are after the Spirit the things of the Spirit. For to be carnally minded is death; but to be spiritually minded is life and peace. Because the carnal mind is enmity against God: for it is not subject to the law of God, neither indeed can be. So then they that are in the flesh cannot please God. But ye are not in the flesh, but in the Spirit, if so be that the Spirit of God dwell in you. Now if any man have not the Spirit of Christ, he is none of his. And if Christ be in you, the body is dead because of sin; but the Spirit is life because of righteousness. But if the Spirit of him that raised up Jesus from the dead dwell in you, he that raised up Christ from the dead shall also quicken your mortal bodies by his Spirit that dwelleth in you. Therefore, brethren, we are debtors, not to the flesh, to live after the flesh. For if ye live after the flesh, ye shall die: but if ye through the Spirit do mortify the deeds of the body, ye shall live. For as many as are led by the Spirit of God, they are the sons of God." Romans 8:1-14 KJV

But what about Him, what about Jesus? He knew what being alone really was. When I look at the cross I do not see three. I see one, one cross. The other two crosses we read about in scripture were the crosses upon which criminals were executed. The cross Jesus was nailed to was the cross I should have been nailed to. In our relationship, the relationship between me and Christ, only One of us was on the cross to pay for my sins. My sins! And in this relationship He was all alone in that payment.

Christ had many days where he was truly not alone yet isolated from His followers. He was arrested, unjustly convicted and sentenced to die on the cross. He was scourged unmercifully. Thorns impaled his brow. He was spat upon, ridiculed and abandoned by His disciples. I expect I would have abandoned Him too. He was going where I could not go. I might like to think that my sacrifice would have done the same thing but it would not. It could not. It took pure blood, the only truly pure blood ever let. My sacrifice would have only achieved death, not life everlasting. But His life, a perfect life, a life without blemish could and would save the world.

And God the Father, how about Him? He was truly and genuinely alone in the experience of His only begotten Son facing death on a cross at the hands of His own creations. A death absolutely undeserved by His Son yet demanded of Him by our actions, our disobedience. It was the way, the only way, and the whole way, the only sacrifice sufficient to redeem the world. The only currency suitable for the price of the world's sins was the blood of the sinless, without blemish, perfect Son of God. The work was all His and He did all the work, alone, quite alone.

We should have all been on that cross with Him. It was my debt being paid. My sentence was carried out on the Son of Almighty God. He had no debt accrued on His own, just mine and yours. But He was alone. None of us were on the cross with Him although every single one of us should have been. It was our death penalty He was serving. And alone He served it. Every time we look on the cross we should see our own image on the cross. But we don't. We see the image of Jesus crucified.

And that's really it isn't it? Christ and Him crucified. That's where salvation was achieved, mine and yours, if you accept what He did. It is the only way you know. And because He did that I will never be alone again, not genuinely alone. He is always with me. And I will always be with Him in the everlasting life He paid for with His own life, His precious blood.

I am never alone....... I will never be alone. No, not ever!

Know ye not that ye are the temple of God, and that the Spirit of God dwelleth in you?
I Corinthians 3:16 KJV

Chapter 3

Give Us Barabbas

A couple of years ago I started studying the New Testament by inspired writer. I started with Paul first primarily because I feel like I understand the man Paul better than the other writers and because of the sheer volume of his writing. I have studied all the New Testament scripture with the exception of Mark which I am presently finishing. John is last but not least. I will begin with John's gospel very soon.

Studying Chapter 15 of Mark yesterday I read of the crowd's chant to release Barabbas instead of Jesus. I have read through this passage many times in my life and listened to others read it during Easter services at church. I have very dramatic televised depictions of this event too. For some reason this time as I read through it I experienced an overwhelming feeling of guilt. I just had to stop and read it over again.

"And straightway in the morning the chief priests held a consultation with the elders and scribes and the whole council, and bound Jesus, and carried him away, and delivered him to Pilate. And Pilate asked him, Art thou the King of the Jews? And he answering said unto him, Thou sayest it. And the chief priests accused him of many things: but he answered nothing. And Pilate asked him again, saying, Answerest thou nothing? behold how many things they witness against thee. But Jesus yet answered nothing; so that Pilate marvelled. Now at that feast he released unto them one prisoner, whomsoever they desired. And there was one named

Barabbas, which lay bound with them that had made insurrection with him, who had committed murder in the insurrection. And the multitude crying aloud began to desire him to do as he had ever done unto them. But Pilate answered them, saying, Will ye that I release unto you the King of the Jews? For he knew that the chief priests had delivered him for envy. But the chief priests moved the people, that he should rather release Barabbas unto them. And Pilate answered and said again unto them, What will ye then that I shall do unto him whom ye call the King of the Jews? And they cried out again, Crucify him. Then Pilate said unto them, Why, what evil hath he done? And they cried out the more exceedingly, Crucify him."
Mark 15:1-14 KJV

During my life I have participated in dramatic presentations at church depicting the scene this very scripture describes. I doubt there have ever been more sinister words uttered than the words "Crucify Him"! During these dramatic reenactments the name Barabbas was shouted and shouted as the people of the day preferred that Jesus should be crucified and Barabbas, a known criminal and insurrectionist should be released. Even during these church events, the name Barabbas just never elicited such a response from me like it did as I studied the Gospel of Mark this week. As a matter of fact, I was silently shouting Barabbas with all I could muster too.

So who was this Barabbas? Maybe you would like to know but I don't really care. What I think is more important is just who really is Barabbas? What is Barabbas and who are all these people screaming for his release and for the crucifixion of Jesus. Why, just why would they do a thing like that, have a murderer released for any reason?

Well the scripture in this passage reveals clearly that the chief priests stirred up the people to turn on Jesus. It was never that Barabbas was such a desirable human being. The chief priests were envious of Jesus and felt threatened by him. So they led the crowd into a frenzy of hatred and envy. This type of behavior is not just first century stuff. It happens all the time. Our politicians engage in it almost as a matter of practice.

Powerful figures have been misleading the masses all through history and it's nearly always driven by envy or the quest for power, one in the same things in this case. The priests were no different. They could not do the things that Jesus could do. The ability to heal and raise the dead and walk on water and command the elements just was not in their bag of tricks. Jesus threatened their standing among the people. But my mind keeps telling me that though I might understand fully enough what the scripture is saying in this text, that there is something else I must realize before moving on to study the entirety of John's inspired writing.

Had I lived in the first century just which side would I have been on? Would I have been calling for the release of Barabbas? I might have yielded to the chief priests and insisted quite loudly for the release of Barabbas and the crucifixion of Jesus. I really just don't know what I would have done. Very likely I would not have even known what was going on at the time. I would like to think I would have pleaded for the release of Jesus but I'm afraid that wouldn't be anything more than overindulging in self worth.

Like now, I have many demands on my time. My life took a turn into unremitting grief and painful disease after my working life in business. All the hours and distractions that were demanded of me were over. My son was killed in an automobile accident just a few hours after I was declared in remission from Wegener's Granulomatosis, a necrotic form of vasculitis, a quite rare disease at that. Three years later I would be terminated from my job, the first such event in my life. And in just a few months a life threatening relapse of vasculitis came calling, taking me out of the workforce permanently.

So the last fifteen years I have studied the Bible, first to understand better the death of my eighteen year old son and then, as I became closer and closer to the eternal aspect of life, I felt I needed to know God better, as intimately as possible. So my study focus shifted from things like heaven and death to just Who is this God that let all this happen? How does He behave and how do I fit into this plan of His? Can I know when He speaks? Can I see Him? Can I know what He expects of me? Is His nature revealed in scripture and deed?

I garden, try to play the banjo, devote much time to my grandson and try to be a better husband and father to my only remaining child on earth, my daughter. I study economics and politics though both subjects seem to be poisonous to the soul. And I write a little dab. Turning back to the writing thing I believe Barabbas was a minor character in this story.

So considering Barabbas, I was less concerned about that man as I read than I was the nameless and faceless members of the crowd voicing their demands for Barabbas so powerfully. I might not have been in that crowd two thousand years ago but I feel a powerful sense of conviction that I am very much in it today. Oh, but I go to church. I don't just sleep through the preaching, my ears are glued to the preacher's words. I really must know more and more about God. It's not a thing about believing either. I believe to a certainty that God has always been. He created all that is and Jesus was there. The first few verses of John's gospel confirm that nothing that was made was made without Jesus. The triune God has always been in all its three parts as One.

Yes, I am way beyond just a hope that there's a God that created you and me. I have been trying to wrap my mind around just what He is for years now. And as much as I have learned I feel like I have only scratched the surface. But scratch on I will. There is so much to know. He gave us instructions on how to live and examples in blood of what happens when we violate His Words. I believe that understanding God better is a very good way to know what to expect from Him in the circumstances we find ourselves during life here on earth. And it's the only way to know what He expects of me.

This whole scene, the demand for Barabbas and the crucifixion of Jesus was no surprise to God. All things are possible for God but I can't remember reading of Him ever being surprised by our actions. Displeasure is found in lots of places in the Bible but surprises are just absent, likely because His omniscience just does not allow for surprise. It's indeed hard to know everything past, present and future all at once and also be surprised by anything. So He is not surprised by my actions but I expect He has been disappointed many times as I stand in the crowd today and scream for Barabbas. Like it or not I expect you're in the crowd with me too.

I might not have been shouting Barabbas in the ears of Pilate but I have shouted many things in the place of Barabbas. The chief priests are not soliciting my action to scream out Barabbas either. It is all me. I am doing my own thinking, experiencing the envy without even realizing it. So I know who Barabbas is to me and it's not the dead for centuries figure the Bible tells me about in Mark 15. It's those things that I would trade for Christ's life without even realizing that's what I am doing.

We hear from nearly every pulpit that we have many idols. They may not be made into the image of a golden calf or be a pole we worship but we have them. We are told that many things have become idolized by us such as wealth, power, fishing and hunting, golf, playing music and anything else that we place before the Lord. But here we are talking about something different. We are not just talking about something that inserts into our lives in the place that Christ should always occupy. We are talking here about literally trading something for the life of Christ in our lives.

This crowd of the first century was actually trading a criminal, a murderer, for the life of the Savior of the World. And this trade involved torture of such unimaginable brutality that it quite frankly escapes my very vivid imagination. They allowed themselves to be incited by the envious chief priests to send the very Son of God to the cross. This trade was less about the release of Barabbas and more about the killing of Jesus. They were not making Barabbas an idol. Truth be told, they probably couldn't stand Barabbas or even worse, didn't even know the trade they were demanding. There was no idol in the form of a human being in this scene. Selfishness, envy and the hatred that arose from both was manifested in the trade for Barabbas with the life of Jesus. Barabbas was no idol. Christ was rejected.

"Then released he Barabbas unto them: and when he had scourged Jesus, he delivered him to be crucified. Then the soldiers of the governor took Jesus into the common hall, and gathered unto him the whole band of soldiers. And they stripped him, and put on him a scarlet robe. And when they had platted a crown of thorns, they put it upon his head, and a reed in his right hand: and they bowed the knee before him, and mocked him, saying, Hail, King of the Jews! And they spit upon him, and took the reed, and smote him on the head. And after that they had mocked him, they took the robe off from him, and put his own raiment on him, and led him away to crucify him. And as they came out, they found a man of Cyrene, Simon by name: him they compelled to bear his cross. And when they were come unto a place called Golgotha, that is to say, a place of a skull, They gave him vinegar to drink mingled with gall: and when he had tasted thereof, he would not drink. And they crucified him, and parted his garments, casting lots: that it might be fulfilled which was spoken by the

prophet, They parted my garments among them, and upon my vesture did they cast lots. And sitting down they watched him there; And set up over his head his accusation written, THIS IS JESUS THE KING OF THE JEWS." Matthew 27:26-37 KJV

So as my mind considered more carefully my role in this trade I must conclude that I have been in the same crowd in this day and time. Have I traded something for the life of Christ? Do I have a Barabbas in my life? Am I so easily misled as to trade the life of the Savior, of Jesus, for something of earthly value, for something of any value? There was a time success meant so much to me that I might have done just that. I have never denied Christ but there have been times, more than I'd like to admit that I would have sacrificed most anything for my own self esteem or notoriety among others.

Indeed, the shouts for Barabbas ring out globally. Created in God's image, how on earth could such selfishness, greed and envy been a part of the triune God. Simply put, choice, our ability to choose our actions must be it, must be that which is within the image of God yet never abused or misused by God. And we abuse it all the time. It's our right as human beings, no? We insist powerfully, even violently, to choose things and to take actions based on our choices that are clearly wrong.

Our "rights" are probably both idols and a substitute version of Barabbas at the same time. We insist on choosing to engage in the act that produces a baby and then claim it's our right to end the "rights" of another human being. And we are out in the street protecting these "rights" at the top of our lungs and by whatever violent means we think we can get away with. I cannot, nor will I, intimate that I know how a woman feels facing that decision. I do know that killing another human being is wrong.

We place ourselves in the place of Christ so frequently these days that I just cannot understand why God has not punished us as He has so many other societies in history. We accommodate the most outlandish claims if the voices are many and loud. We will swear a lie to accommodate "unity". Rest assured there is no unity to be found in dishonesty. We codify immorality and protect practices that are simply forbidden in scripture and defy common sense too.

We make bad decisions because we are not continually grounding ourselves in scripture, in His Word. It's a lifetime practice to stay focused on what God would have us do, how He would have us behave and what choices are prescribed by His Holy Word. It takes a dedication to prayer, study about and focus on God, to understand Him better and better all the time and to execute on His will for our lives.

I am not going to spend any more time here on this. But what have we traded for Jesus? What have we accepted in place of the Sacrifice made for us? What are we shouting for? I hope, I will try to stay out of the crowds, I will even try to avoid acting alone, pleading for anything in the place of Jesus.

What shall we do with Jesus?

Chapter 4

An Angel Before Thee

"And I will send an angel before thee; and I will drive out the Canaanite, the Amorite, and the Hittite, and the Perizzite, the Hivite, and the Jebusite: Unto a land flowing with milk and honey: for I will not go up in the midst of thee; for thou art a stiffnecked people: lest I consume thee in the way."
   Exodus 33:2-3 KJV

How many times has an angel been sent to do one thing or another for God? I heard this passage preached not long ago and as usual my focus upon review of the passage was to exactly what the sermon was about. Sometimes, very often indeed, my attention finds the more obscure clauses to be a point that captivates my interest and spurs my imagination. And plural versus singular usage makes a powerful difference in my understanding of things revealed to us. Just like this passage in Exodus chapter 33 where God tells Moses that He will send an angel before him. An angel, now that's one, one angel. That seems like a mighty task for a legion of angels yet God sends one angel.

The extent of the power of angels is really unknown to us in totality. I suspect that we would have a very different view of angels if we really knew. God, of course, does know and sends one angel on the epic course to follow. We know what happened here. History records the events that follow. The angels aren't mentioned so prominently in history, if at all, but this passage subtly speaks so powerfully as to the power given by God to one angel. One angel with such power, totally lacking in the descriptive adjectives preceding the noun, is indicative of the power and glory exhibited by angels.

There are other passages in the Bible that do reflect, at least in some small way, the glory and power of angels in force. The book of Revelation is full of angelic action of global power. When Elisha asked that his servant's eyes be opened to behold the great force around them, they were described as "horses and chariots of fire", Exodus 6:17 KJV. A whole mountain full of angelic beings, horses and chariots of fire around and about them was certainly an overwhelmingly powerful and glorious force. There are many instances of the power of angels and God's use of them in accomplishing His will. It really sets my imagination on fire to think of the untold times that God has used angels in my life, and in larger focus, in the history of the world.

Imagination is not always a healthy thing to engage, especially in studying the Bible. I believe I tend to interpret things within my will rather than that of God's will. But engage it I will. It's the only way I can appreciate the power of God in my mind aside from study alone. The Bible tells us that we might have entertained angels unaware. I suspect I have done that very thing sometime in the past, maybe many times, and maybe it wasn't so entertaining for the angels. I hope in heaven that there is a class like Angels 590, you know, a graduate course for those who are fascinated by angels, have thought on them quite a lot, and desire even after death to fully appreciate the creatures we have winged and made into harp players.

In the Exodus 33 passage an angel is sent. I take that literally to be an angel, one angel. The tasks at hand for the angel would likely be a daunting one for a whole army of mere mortals heavily armed. But God sends an angel. Even more subtle is that no mention is made of the angel by name. So it wasn't like Michael was sent, an angel that should strike a strong fear of

God in us all. It was just an angel. It was just an angel sent to prepare the way for entry into the Promised Land. Michael, when disputing the devil, remarked that he would leave his rebuke to the Lord. It kind of comes off as the more powerful angel not wanting to waste the time on the devil even though he had the power to chastise him heavily. There is certainly nothing to indicate that the angel Michael fears anything, even the devil.

Angels are important beings. Created beings, there is no indication that they procreate. In fact, we are told in scripture that we will be like angels in certain regards though we will not be angels. And one of those traits is that we will not procreate in heaven. We do not know whether God makes more angels all the time or even if there is a finite number. I really don't think it is important how many angels exist. We do know from scripture that some fell with Lucifer strongly suggesting that they do have free will. The evidence suggests to me that the majority of them exercise their free will quite wisely, unlike God's human creations that share a few attributes with the angels.

So aside from the cited actions of God's use for angels in scriptures, my mind takes off through my world of events, minor and major, where angels might have been involved. I try not to focus on terms like guardian angel. I tend to focus more, as does the Exodus passage, on the more subtle term "an angel". So in my life where does chance stop and supernatural intervention begin and do the two occur together? Chance, a term I think we use to explain that which we cannot explain, I believe plays far less a role in our lives than supernatural, angelic assistance. I do not believe God uses angels to circumvent the free will He chose to gives us. It would not really be free will if He intervened directly. I do believe He uses angelic action to influence us.

The inaudible voice, is that the voice of an angel? Is it the voice of the Holy Spirit? They are not the same, an angel and the Holy Spirit. The Holy Spirit is the third Person in the Trinity, coequal with the Father and the Son. Angels are not God, not even a part of the Trinity. I believe the powerful, inaudible voice I hear is that of the Holy Spirit, promised to me and indwelling in me. That one might think that to be an absurd belief just indicates that I don't always listen to that voice though I should without fail. So I don't believe angels have that kind of power over us, that kind of divine influence. I think they can have their way with us in even matters of life and death and in accomplishing the will of God yet I don't think they can overrule our free choice that God enabled within us all.

As in the death of my son, his actions, choices he made within his God given ability to choose, even if unwisely, were uninfluenced by angels. But at the same time I believe the actions of angels probably were exercised that day to prevent more serious injury to three of the other occupants of the vehicle in which Alex was killed. And even though Alex was killed, the influence of angels likely spared him much pain and suffering as his injuries were fatal in plurality. Protection was likely afforded by angels to the residents where the accident took place. I believe that was quite likely.

And just after the accident, the calm that fell over me, I just have to wonder if angels effected an environment of calm whilst we struggled to acclimate to such a horrendous loss. Who did God send? How many did God send? Was it the action of angels or the hedge of protection from the Holy Spirit? I've always known that whether by angels, the Holy Spirit or whatever other heavenly source, all good things come from God. I believe that even if angels are the executors, they are still only acting within the framework given them directly by God. They are not autonomous creatures acting upon their own thoughts and desires. I believe that when scripture intimates that we will be like the angels that one of those attributes will be that we will always be acting within the will of God freely, that our actions will be entirely those pleasing to God. As is true here, God's will is not forced on us. No, it's that when heaven is a personal reality, when we really see Him, when it's a sight walk, our free choice will follow within the glory of God in our new home, the one He went to prepare. I think that is one way we will be like angels.

Will it not be wonderful to be acting entirely, one hundred percent, without fail, always and forever within the will of God as our free choice and act! Here, before crossing the veil of death, that is just something we as Christians try to do. We fail miserably. Some might suggest we are humanly incapable for choosing infallibly within the will of God. I don't believe that for a minute. If we are capable of choosing one thing within His will we are capable of choosing another, and another and another and another. We just choose not to for a variety of almost limitless reasons. It makes me feel good. It is financially wise. It makes me look better than I am. It elevates my appearance to the world around me. It's physically gratifying. Those are just a few of the motivations for our choices that would be considered worthy to us in making choices outside the will of God. In a few words, it is sin in our lives, in my life.

So will that image, what I see when face to Face with God, be so powerful that it alone corrects the flaws in our exercise of free will? You bet! It's kept the most of the angels in line even without the relationship that we have with God. He sent His Son to reconcile me to Him. He didn't even do that for the angels. He did it for me. Such a powerful price was paid by Him for me that I believe that we scarcely scratch the surface of the appreciation we should have for it while here in our present body. But we could. It is so that we just make choices that are so flawed by cheap and temporary influences.

I stray from the point. I can't help it. It does all culminate at the cross and I just can't keep from going there while I try to mindfully examine actions of angels in my life. Another time in my life was life threatening and I wondered about the influence of angels in my life. Like this disease I have, Wegener's Granulomatosis, a disease most have never heard of and could care less about. Most doctors will likely never see a case of this type of incurable vasculitis. Though it's a rare and incurable disease, one popularly described as invisible, it can be quite deadly while being managed quite effectively. To look at me you wouldn't suspect the vulnerability I have to regular everyday things. Decisions that require careful consideration and advice are not even decisions for you normal mortals. When and how much red meat can I have? Am I properly hydrating? Is my blood pressure under control? Does what I'm eating contain too much salt? Diet is a big deal with scarred kidneys and the prospect for further damage certain.

And it's not only my diet that's critical, physical actions can prove life threatening to me. The use of a chain saw would be considered absolutely insane for me with low platelets and a depressed immune system. It has taken my immune system more than ten years to get to a point where I am considered barely normal as to risk of infection and my ability to fight infection. A fall for you might result in a bruise while the same fall for me might result in an uncontrollable hemorrhage that ends in death. I would suggest to you that I try to balance the risks of leading as near normal a life as I can with the risks of grave injury and death. And lately I have entertained the thought that angels are likely involved in the duty of protection of me from outside perils, ending that day God chooses to let my choices play out in my future end on earth.

What accidents were prevented by an angel while on my way to an infusion? What virus was I isolated from by an angel? When have I fallen that an angel lessened the impact. What factors, countless threats, have I been protected from by an angel. An angel! An angel acting on instructions from God! I am less inclined to focus on an angel acting as a guardian against all perils in the duty of protection of this writer and more inclined to believe the actions of an angel are always, without fail or reason, upon the direct instructions from God. He, God, has some reason, within His will, for my still being here. God has choices too. But His are always right.

We so fear death that I think we would fall victim to the suggestion that death might be avoided. Perish the thought. I will die. You will die. One would think that if an angel is a guardian that the angel failed in its duties if death results. Could an angel fail? That is very doubtful if not totally absurd to say the least. That's why I do not believe they are here to guard against calamity but rather to act within the will of God for His sole purposes. And sometimes that might even result in our death. Natural disasters, plane crashes, lightning strikes and many other things can result in our death through no direct fault of our own. Where is an angel during these events? They are there. As was true in Elisha's time, they are all around us though we probably, almost certainly, are not their primary focus. They serve God, whatever He would have for them to do. Could it be that we are just indirect beneficiaries of their actions while acting on behalf of almighty God? Maybe, but I believe it can be both. I believe an angel or angels have acted to my personal benefit at times while an angel has also prevented me from larger calamity like an earthquake.

An angel, let's elevate this singular use of the beings we think of and scripture refers to as angels. An agent of God, an action noun for use as God chooses, not necessarily here for my personal benefit. To suggest that an angel is here just for my benefit seems to lessen their role in the Kingdom of God. We are such selfish creatures that we would suggest, if even only privately to ourselves, that angels are here for our personal concerns and protection. And doubtless, the effects of an angel in our lives would certainly lend to that belief. But our lives pass just like a vapor. Seems I've read that somewhere before. Of course I have and anyone that has studied the Bible in the least is familiar with that. So I think we should take a closer look at an angel in our lives so as to gain understanding on just what is paramount in the moment by moment life of an angel.

The power of angels, an angel, cannot be overstated yet it, as is true even for Satan, is limited to that power ordained by God. They are not all powerful. It might seem as if they are in comparison to the power we as human beings command. So just as in the case of an angel in Exodus 33, the subtlety of the reference of an angel in relation to the task given the angel should display the power of just an angel, really just "an" angel. Understatement can sometimes accent the larger display of just a few words. "And I will send an angel before thee", an angel.

Lastly, just take a few minutes to envision, yes with your imagination, what the shepherds saw that night. It was the angelic announcement of the coming Messiah. Signifying the eternal importance of the coming event, God sent the angels, a whole multitude of angels.

"And there were in the same country shepherds abiding in the field, keeping watch over their flock by night. And, lo, the angel of the Lord came upon them, and the glory of the Lord shone round about them: and they were sore afraid.. And the angel said unto them, Fear not: for, behold, I bring you good tidings of great joy, which shall be to all people. For unto you is born this day in the city of David a Saviour, which is Christ the Lord. And this shall be a sign unto you; Ye shall find the babe wrapped in swaddling clothes, lying in a manger. And suddenly there was with the angel a multitude of the heavenly host praising God, and saying, Glory to God in the highest, and on earth peace, good will toward men. And it came to pass, as the angels were gone away from them into heaven, the shepherds said one to another, Let us now go even unto Bethlehem, and see this thing which is come to pass, which the Lord hath made known unto us. And they came with haste,

and found Mary, and Joseph, and the babe lying in a manger."
Luke 2:8-16 KJV.

More than an angel, a whole host of heavenly beings appeared to the shepherds during this announcement of the birth of Jesus in nearby Bethlehem. An angel, the power of one angel was used for the Israelites to enter the Promised Land. A whole multitude of heavenly hosts were present to announce this birth, the birth that would bring the Savior of the world to earth. Was this angelic display significant? I think it goes to a measure of the event. The entry of the Israelites into the Promised Land after forty years wandering in the desert and four hundred years of captivity was attended to by an angel. In comparison, there is no more important event than the life of Christ from birth all the way to His resurrection.

There are so many events in Jesus' life that John opined that the whole world might not hold the books were they all recorded. The birth, life, death and resurrection of Jesus remain a divinely masterful event in the singular and a seemingly infinite collection of things He did while here. Jesus, the Christ, more than an angel. The power displayed to the shepherds must've been almost beyond belief judging by the power of just an angel.

Indeed, just an angel.

Chapter 5

Who Did It

I am fascinated by the intricacy of things, really all things. I am beyond trying to learn very much about these things. I suppose I have reached the point in life that I now have just about all the useful information I need to lead my life to a successful entry into everlasting life at the pearly gates. Occasionally something comes up that I have a need for new information. I have a few hobbies that have moved from the learning how phase well into the maintenance phase. I am a vegetable gardener, a beekeeper, a banjo player and a fair to middlin' grandpa to the best grandson in the world, EVER! I very much love being on the tractor throughout the year and I do just about all my tractor maintenance myself. With the exception of gardening, I already know just about all I am interested in knowing in order to work within these hobbies. But just about all my searches for new information, for new knowledge, are not focused on the how-to nearly as much as the "who-did-it".

I am fascinated with the very small, those things that exist that are too small to see with the naked eye yet they exist and are integral to the workings of the world, indeed life itself. In high school fifty years ago we briefly studied the atom. It seems that there is a lot going on in the atom and immense power is contained within. I don't pretend to know very much about the atom but my fascination with it comes from the "who-did-it" aspect, particularly the Who-did-it. One must admit that design is clearly evident everywhere whether you believe the creation account in Genesis or not. When I was first exposed to the atom, I suppose in physics class, the things I drew from it were few. But I did form a question right away. Just who did it? This couldn't possibly have occurred by accident. With all the activity happening all the time in the atom many questions arise but none more important that who did it. I didn't really get much into that question at the time. At that point in my life I was just concerned about passing tests, going fishing and paying attention to my girlfriend.

And then there is the super large, those gargantuan things, most of which we still cannot see. There are planets, stars and galaxies so large yet so distant that they are only a pinpoint of light in our vision if even visible at all. I have owned a couple telescopes in my life. One was a really good telescope and I could see Mars, Jupiter and Saturn coming through the optics of this instrument. This telescope, once zoomed in on the subject, could track the object as the earth rotated. Much must be known for this telescope to perform that task. It must be programmed with the precise latitude and longitude. It must be programmed with the precise speed and direction within which the earth rotates and orbits the sun. It is quite a piece of work. And what did I find out that was useful? Not much. But I knew who did it. Watching these distant objects at distances beyond my normal ability to see while observing their color and isolation within the solar system just brings to question who did it.

And actions, so many things have actions they repeat from one year to the next. How do squirrels know cold weather is coming and store up food for those times? Why do some species of fish swim treacherous waters, defying waterfalls, to spawn every year at the same time? Why does the purple martin come to my birdhouse gourd hanging just off the corner of the garden year after year? And why do they leave so early? And why do they choose a dried out old gourd within which to live and raise their young? And how does the seed keep growing these gourds in the same shape every year for thousands of years? Is it Divinity looking over it all? I just don't know. Again, Who did it?

"Behold the fowls of the air: for they sow not, neither do they reap, nor gather into barns; yet your heavenly Father feedeth them. Are ye not much better than they?" Matthew 6:26 KJV

Why does the limestone fail in its resistance to flowing water? Why does some limestone have colorful crystals within its outer shell and why is the rest just plain old limestone, crushed for use on driveways and country lanes? Why is water not exhausted after first use? Truly forever renewable, water is one of the very forces of nature, of creation, that is vital to sustain life. The earth is the perfect spaceship. Set in motion during the act of creation, it has maintained its motion ever since. And so has this movement remained an attribute of all the other space bodies. It provides the environment to sustain life literally in perpetuity. The atmosphere protects its inhabitants from nearly all intruders, visible or not. And why are the orbits of comets so different than that of the planets? And what is this invisible attachment all things have to these gravity exerting bodies? I mean really, who did that? And why so many celestial bodies if only earth is inhabited? The ocean tides? Tornadoes, snow and rain, hot and cold, just who did that? Who did it?

Why do Canada geese mate for life? Few species are monogamous. Humans are monogamous, much evidence appears to be to the contrary. Theories abound from both the educated and the uneducated. As a beekeeper I am often tempted when asked why bees do certain things to say, "Well, the bees think so and so". Really and truly I'm quite certain I haven't a clue what the bees think. I can only observe what they do and offer theories as to what they might be thinking. It is possible bees don't think at all. It's possible they are programmed to behave a certain way and their brains are just guidance devices. I choose to believe that honey bees think but

I don't really know that. But I do know this, they do the same routine from one year to the next and make the most delicious honey. Who determined their routine, what works for them?

And the blueprint for a human being, DNA, screams design. It is common knowledge that DNA contains millions if not billions of bits of information. Furthermore, each person's DNA is unique to that individual. It determines, even before birth our appearance, tendencies to contract certain diseases, the color of our hair and eyes or the absence of either. It's the lifelong house plans for this physical body that serves as transportation for the heart and mind and soul. I have always wondered why we were not all made alike. It would have simplified things a whole lot. The same blood type would have made transplants much more widely available. But it's the lack of an identically homogeneous mankind that lends beauty to the species. He did that!

Those that argue that life sprang forth from an explosion from nothingness must ignore the evidence of design and the inner workings of the species on the space body we hurtle through space on. Some just flee from the thought that there is a greater Being than themselves. I believe it did come from nothingness but not by explosion. It came from nothingness by the spoken word of almighty God, perfectly within HIs infinite Being and perfect ability. Indeed, He did that just as the Bible tells us He did.

"In the beginning God created the heaven and the earth. And the earth was without form, and void; and darkness was upon the face of the deep. And the Spirit of God moved upon the face of the waters. And God said, Let there be light: and there was light. And God saw the light, that it was good: and God divided the light from the darkness. And God called the light Day, and the darkness he called Night. And the evening and the morning were the first day. And God said, Let there be a firmament in the midst of the waters, and let it divide the

waters from the waters. And God made the firmament, and divided the waters which were under the firmament from the waters which were above the firmament: and it was so. And God called the firmament Heaven. And the evening and the morning were the second day. And God said, Let the waters under the heaven be gathered together unto one place, and let the dry land appear: and it was so. And God called the dry land Earth; and the gathering together of the waters called he Seas: and God saw that it was good. And God said, Let the earth bring forth grass, the herb yielding seed, and the fruit tree yielding fruit after his kind, whose seed is in itself, upon the earth: and it was so. And the earth brought forth grass, and herb yielding seed after his kind, and the tree yielding fruit, whose seed was in itself, after his kind: and God saw that it was good. And the evening and the morning were the third day. And God said, Let there be lights in the firmament of the heaven to divide the day from the night; and let them be for signs, and for seasons, and for days, and years: And let them be for lights in the firmament of the heaven to give light upon the earth: and it was so. And God made two great lights; the greater light to rule the day, and the lesser light to rule the night: he made the stars also. And God set them in the firmament of the heaven to give light upon the earth, And to rule over the day and over the night, and to divide the light from the darkness: and God saw that it was good. And the evening and the morning were the fourth day. And God said, Let the waters bring forth abundantly the moving creature that hath life, and fowl that may fly above the earth in the open firmament of heaven. And God created great whales, and every living creature that moveth, which the waters brought forth abundantly, after their kind, and every winged fowl after his kind: and God saw that it was good. And God blessed them, saying, Be fruitful, and multiply, and fill the waters in the seas, and let fowl multiply in the earth. And the evening and the morning were the fifth day. And God said, Let the earth bring forth the living creature after his kind, cattle, and creeping thing, and beast of the earth after his kind: and it *was so. And God made the beast of the earth after his kind, and cattle after their kind, and every thing that creepeth upon the earth after his kind: and God saw that it was good. And God said, Let us make man in our image, after our likeness: and let them have dominion over the fish of the sea, and over the fowl of the air, and over the cattle, and over all the earth, and over every creeping thing that creepeth upon the earth. So God created man in his own image, in the image of God created he him; male and female created he them. And God blessed them, and God said unto them, Be fruitful, and multiply, and replenish the earth, and subdue it: and have dominion over the fish of the sea, and over the fowl of the air, and over every living thing that moveth upon the earth. And God said, Behold, I have given you every herb bearing seed, which is upon the face of all the earth, and every tree, in the which is the fruit of a tree yielding seed; to you it shall be for meat. And to every beast of the earth, and to every fowl of the air, and to every thing that creepeth upon the earth, wherein there is life, I have given every green herb for meat: and it was so. And God saw every thing that he had made, and, behold, it was very good. And the evening and the morning were the sixth day." Genesis 1:1-31 KJV*

Aging, the unavoidable destiny of our minds and physical bodies is another miracle of life and one that fascinates me. As undesirable as aging is there are benefits that tag along with the process of aging. I think I make better decisions in my sixties than in my forties. My level of patience far exceeds what it was during my working life. My ability to listen to the problems, concerns and comments of others is finally at the level of that of a compassionate person. I am not so judgmental and I can't think of a single person I hate. Rather, I like human beings even generally speaking, even those I disagree with strenuously. Most people I would probably not choose to spend a day on the lake with but I still see value in all people. Years ago I respected most those that were successful businessmen. Age and better judgment has changed that. I now respect those whose devotion to scripture and spiritual endeavors is clearly visible in their lives. Accordingly, I find the counterfeit versions of these spiritual giants quite distasteful.

Why do we age comparatively quickly as compared to the age of say, a sequoia tree? Who did this? I would make the argument that our physical bodies, even our brain harbored minds, were designed and created to live forever. Had there been no original sin, there would have been no need for a Savior and the absence of death would have been here just as it is in heaven. But the exercise of free will combined with temptation and envy entered the picture and the penalty was death. God, knowing everything as I believe to a certainty He does, knowing all of history and all of the future knew a Savior would be required. Omniscience comes in handy when your life or the lives of those you love come into question. I have heard those that suggest that God failed in His first attempt and had to send His Son to serve as a sacrifice for those that would repent and believe on Him. I do not believe that at all. Had God ever failed at anything he would not be God. But still the complexity of the simplicity of the entire story of God-created civilization is so easy to grasp yet avoided by so many. Who did that?

You must be asking yourself, at least I am hoping that you are, just why God did not create a perfect mankind, avoiding the whole sin and sacrifice thing, thereby avoiding the need for the sacrifice of His only Son? I must admit, I looked for the answer to that question for years when at last I found it had stared me in the face nearly all my life. God loved the world so much that He gave His only begotten Son to save the world. Ever heard of John 3:16? There was no mistake. Giving one's life was the ultimate show of love. By just creating mankind in a perfect form would have shown a love but not with the same depth that leaving heaven and coming to earth to die as a sacrifice for those you love does, the ultimate show of love. He did that!

And the many ways that life continues on this planet captured my attention as my parents aged and eventually died. The human body is often a tough thing to kill while still being quite fragile. My father died in his early eighties after enduring multiple surgeries throughout his life for heart disease related ailments and hernias. He finally succumbed to complications of treatments for lung cancer. My mother lived a few years longer but the cause of death on her death certificate reads "failure to thrive". They both lived long, productive lives. Dad had heart issues for thirty years and mom suffered from debilitating rheumatoid arthritis, diabetes and finally, dementia. My oldest sister's husband died of brain cancer five and half years into a six to nine months life expectancy. His last day seemed like he was engaged in such a struggle to die. It took all day. He fought to the very end. In that way he was a hero. Disease seems to take a long, arduous way with the end of our lives. Then on the other hand, my son died as nearly instantly as I would like to believe, having crashed his pickup into a tree. He was just eighteen years old at his death.

That last death I have struggled with for nearly fourteen years. A death like that is hard to understand considering God looks over us. One expects the elder to go first. If God knows everything that has happened, happening now and ever will happen, and I believe He does, then why does he not intervene? Could He not have spared my mother and father the suffering and allowed them death a bit earlier? Could He not have restored my son to his six foot three framed picture of health? I fully believe He could. But then I yield to His planning when I think on all He has done and I acknowledge that His way must be better. I mourned for all three. Admittedly, I still mourn for my son even though I know he is in heaven in the very presence of God. Did God fail me?

And grief, why do we grieve so at the loss of one so close? Why is the loss of a child so devastating, indeed life enduring? It would seem that grief is mostly, if not entirely, confined to human beings. Grief, of course, is mostly not a tangible thing though it can produce devastating actions that affect physical things, other human beings and essentially ruin one's life. Grief driven people can commit violent acts or engage in self harm, even the act of taking a life. It seems that deep depression is often associated with prolonged grief. Speaking from personal experience I just withdrew from about everything and engaged in deep study of Heaven and why bad things happen to good people. I expect I wouldn't have learned the things I learned without grief being the motivator. Where did our ability to grieve come from? Other species might grieve but I expect that until they can speak a language we can understand I will assert that grief is a God given ability unique to mankind.

And in addition to this scratching of the natural world's, the created world's, surface that I have given words to in this chapter, very likely the tie that binds it all together is the ability to love. Not only can we show love, we can sense love when shown to us. We can withhold love. We can personify love by our actions. Love drowns hatred. Hatred makes for a miserable human being. I have personally seen the harbors of both love and hatred within my own family. The effects of hatred are devastatingly vicious. Jealousy driven hatred has cost the lives of many and the happiness of all exposed to it. But on the other hand, love is a soothing act benefiting both the lover and the loved. And it is the love of God for the species He created in His image that saves us from ourselves. But we have a choice. One must acknowledge and repent for the sin in one's life and believe that God's very own Son came and died to save us from the penalty of sin. Love indeed. That is the love of God. He did it. God did it.

Indeed, God did it all, He is responsible for it all and He gave His all for His image bearers.

God did it!

Chapter 6

Figuring Out the Bad Things

So what about the bad things? Didn't God promise that all things would be used for good for those that love Him? Maybe that's what He said in scripture. I'm not going to tell you but a few things that God said about the bad things. I am going to speak mostly from experience as I most often have had to do. I have had plenty of "bad" things happen in my life. At least I thought they were bad things. I have had more than my share of good things too. The good things don't seem to concern us nearly as much as the bad things. Don't they both come from the same place? Or do they? Does God engineer some of our misfortune? Certainly, God tests us from time to time. Some of these tests are all but unnoticeable and others stick out among only a few milestones in our lives here on earth.

"My brethren, count it all joy when ye fall into divers temptations; Knowing this, that the trying of your faith worketh patience. But let patience have her perfect work, that ye may be perfect and entire, wanting nothing. If any of you lack wisdom, let him ask of God, that giveth to all men liberally, and upbraideth not; and it shall be given him."
James 1:2-5 KJV

My earliest memories go back to childhood. It seemed I was prone to fractures of my bones. I broke an arm twice, a thumb once and my collar bone was apparently broken in childbirth. Of course I don't remember that break but as you can see, I am no stranger to bones breaking. In an effort to help a friend once when his father was having heart problems, I contracted histoplasmosis from the excrement of chickens, a life threatening fungal infection of the lungs. Unlike the painful bone fractures, which were painful for sure, histoplasmosis was both painful and made me wonder if I just might die. I was about eighteen at the time and a stranger to farm equipment. I grew up on a farm but the only thing cheap about dad was our farm equipment. We never had a tractor, just a riding mower and a front tine tiller. We built fences on the farm out of the trunk of an Oldsmobile Delta 88.

My bone fractures healed more slowly than the fractures of other children. And frankly, I was a non compliant patient when it came to physical therapy once the casts were removed. Squeezing a tennis ball or carrying around a bucket of rocks all day just was not appealing enough for me to buckle down to rebuild the strength in my arms and thumb. I was too young during the fractures to wonder about whether or not they were a God thing or not. In fact, carelessness could be traced to the cause of all three of my childhood fractures. There didn't seem to be a heavenly message in any of it at the time. But my lack of compliance with the post recovery therapy resulted in smaller wrists and less arm strength than other adults of my size and weight. I have concentrated on moderate weight training all my adult life but it didn't come from the message of the broken bones.

Early in my working life I ignored just about everything except my job. I was successful in getting a job with an independent oil exploration company right out of school. It was 1980 and the national economy was reeling from high interest rates, high inflation and high unemployment. Entry level jobs were hard to come by. I was fortunate to get the job even though the starting salary was below what my graduating college buddies were starting at. The job allowed me to stay in close proximity to where I grew up and to raise a family in the rurality of middle Tennessee. I had trained in school to be a bank examiner but

President Carter cut many of the new hires from the FDIC just two weeks before I graduated.

There I was, twenty two years old, married and had no job just two weeks before graduation. All my classmates had one thing I didn't have: a job. I remember wondering if God was punishing me for something. Of course when I got the job the thought that God was in that just didn't enter my mind. I was so glad I was able to finally get a job. My first day of work was on a Saturday, in fact, it was graduation day which I missed for the job. I didn't at the time, nor do I now, consider missing the graduation ceremony a loss in life. I had turned the page from education to climbing the ladder. And though I didn't know it at the time, this drilling company let me do things others thirty years my senior only dreamed of doing, gaining valuable experience. I excelled. I put in the time too, often working sixty or seventy hours in a week, week in and week out. I was salaried but not a clock watcher. I was just in need of making more money. I neglected my family. I missed a lot of time with my wife that I would love to have back

I was picking up bad habits just as soon as I saw how cool they appeared. So the bad habits, the work ethic and a sedentary lifestyle produced a chronic back problem. It was painful and I thought I must have a slipped disk or had developed a bulging disk or cancer or anything else that was less than a self inflicted illness. Was God speaking to me? Maybe He was. But I am more inclined to think that I was feeling the results, the fruits, really the bad fruits of my decisions. In retrospect, I never looked at either the problem or the solution as a God thing. I knew what I had been doing and had already figured out that I must have suffered lasting damage as a result of bad choices and practices. And it was hurting my family too. My wife was very dissatisfied and now we had a little girl trying to look up to daddy. I'm really not satisfied with the role model I provided for my children.

My back issues went from bad to worse as I took in various prescription strength drugs to relieve the swelling that was thought by the orthopedic doctors to be causing my pain. About all the strong anti-inflammatory drugs did for me was produce heartburn and a false sense that I would soon get better. The more pain I was in the more I looked for solutions. I used a special lumbar support office chair and I had a lumbar cushion for driving. The more I tried solutions that were not effective the harder I sought relief. This went on not for weeks or months but for years. I was eating Tylenol like candy for headaches, anti inflammatory drugs for back pain and drinking coffee by the pot. I was slowly killing myself, a result of poor decisions. And I was working pretty hard at doing so.

But all of it eventually added up to a solution and I do think it was a God thing, a good thing too. One day a friend suggested that I see a client of his that was a physiatrist. Now read that label physiatrist carefully so as not to confuse it with psychiatrist which I probably needed as well. The physiatrist did a thorough and careful physical examination after reviewing x-rays and other pertinent information from my family doctor. He explained to me that surgery would correct my situation but greatly limit the flexibility of my back. He also indicated that he wasn't inclined to recommend multiple vertebra fusions for someone of my young age. He said that eighty percent of those complaining with chronic back pain would have surgery yet only twenty percent really needed surgical correction. He explained to me how the weight of the body is distributed and which muscles carry the load. One visit and about three years of really, really painful self therapy at home based on his instructions provided total relief. Since that time, well over thirty years ago, I have rarely had much, well let's call it discomfort because it really wasn't true pain. But I have continued much of his recommendations all my life since that first visit.

Was it a God thing that I listened to this doctor? I think it was but probably not what most people would it expect it to be. The problem was caused entirely by poor decisions, bad habits and a sedentary lifestyle. I chose them, the bad choices, and I knew better. And I would not go as far as to say that the physiatrist was a God thing either. The whole thing God used for good. Even throughout this time I did love God yet I neglected God more even than my family. Many were the times I called out to God to make it all better but I don't quite recall suggesting to God that I would do my part. No, I just wanted relief, unilateral relief, the kind of relief that would allow me to continue down a self destructive path. If the physiatrist did anything for me, he suggested that I wouldn't have the willpower to comply with his instructions. That challenge set me on a path to recovery, long lasting recovery. I am just like most people. I will take the easy road when it is available. But this time the doctor seemed to challenge my discipline and willpower.

So what was God's involvement if He deserves any credit at all? God respected the very free will He gave me and I believe He would've let me pull out enough rope to hang myself. But without a doubt, the strength to rehabilitate myself came from Him and Him alone. I had lived all my life avoiding discipline. He gave me the circumstances, the strength and the discipline to recover once free will involved my looking to Him. He said draw near to Him and He would draw near to me. He gave us, he gave me, instructions on how to live. He said not to kill, bear witness falsely, or not to steal among other things. But most of all He commanded that we, that I, love Him above all else. There were many things on the top of my list but loving God above all else had slipped a good bit. Throughout the recovery process I continually compared my choices with God's commandments until I reached the conclusions that what God had to say to me through scripture was not just a few suggestions. Indeed not, they were what He expected from us, from me. And they were not just take it or leave it things either. They were the things we would be judged by when judgment day comes. Did my failure to acknowledge God's instructions cause my back problem? Of course it did. My priorities were of a single mind. I wanted to excel at my chosen profession and make money. That has been a struggle all my life but I made room for God closer to the top of the list.

"Submit yourselves therefore to God. Resist the devil, and he will flee from you. Draw nigh to God, and he will draw nigh to you. Cleanse your hands, ye sinners; and purify your hearts, ye double minded. Be afflicted, and mourn, and weep: let your laughter be turned to mourning, and your joy to heaviness. Humble yourselves in the sight of the Lord, and he shall lift you up." James 4:7-10 KJV

Finally, I got the priorities more closely aligned with the prescription God has for us. A couple of decades passed then pain returned to me. This time it was very different. The pain moved around a good bit. The back pain earlier in life was a dull, constant pain that radiated down the backs of my legs. The back issue was painful for sure but the pain I was facing now as I approached fifty years old was excruciating. It attacked a couple of joints at a time over three years until it finally made a home in my large joints. Walking was difficult and at times I used a cane to keep me working and ambulatory. But the pain only got worse with each passing day. I was referred to a neurologist because the back issues earlier in life were suspected as having returned with a vengeance. She found nothing to cause the pain and suggested it was probably muscular pain. Then a rheumatologist diagnosed me with rheumatoid arthritis and prescribed strong anti inflammatory drugs and believe me, these drugs caused as many problems as they were meant to help.

Diagnostics included just about everything, everything but a urinalysis. After every life insurance company rejected my application for a life insurance policy the doctors finally had something else to explore. There was blood in my urine. I tried to explain it away as a complication of rheumatoid arthritis but the insurance companies would have none of it. They just flatly refused to cover me at any price for any amount until an answer to the blood in my urine was found. Into the health threat enters the nephrologist, the kidney specialist. He gave comfort and encouragement while we awaited all new lab results. It was thought that an infection or other treatable condition would be found to be the culprit. But a few weeks into diagnosis and a pathology report for a kidney biopsy later, when asked what the result was, he replied, "It's the worst possible news". I had microscopic polyangiitis, a rare form of vasculitis, which is essentially swelling of the small blood vessels.

Well great! We had our explanation finally, about three years into the pain. The diagnosis of what was causing the blood in my urine, the unremitting pain and a generally growing feeling that I would die was finally in. This disease was usually fatal in about five months without treatment and treatment for the disease was pretty new. It attacked my kidneys inflicting permanent damage. I have about fifty percent of the kidney function as does a healthy person with normal kidneys. The chronic kidney disease stage is 3b after drifting in and out of stage 4 a couple times. That's bad. The treatment took six months and lots of steroids but I was put into remission in April 2011. So I have said enough about the disease. That's been fourteen years since entering a remission of sorts. So I will tell you how I think God used this disease for my good and the good of others.

Unlike my back problems from early in adulthood, there was nothing to indicate that my choices or lifestyle contributed to this disease. The doctors didn't know where it came from just that it came. But I suspected right away that God was working with this disease. I didn't know quite what he would do with it but it's been fourteen years since first remission so I have been able to observe a lot. After the first treatment period, well, exactly on the day I was pronounced in remission, my son was killed instantly in an automobile accident that also claimed the life of his friend, another occupant of his pickup truck. Others sustained serious injury. From the point of remission on I believe that the start of relapse came with his death. After about three years I lost my job as chief executive officer of a national sporting goods manufacturer and importer. I was getting sicker by the minute and within a year I would be back on steroids and taking weekly infusions to attempt to induce remission again. That was ten years ago. I knew it was more serious this time. Quoting the nephrologist this time, "I'm afraid that if the disease doesn't kill you the treatment will."

The struggle to recover was tough. For more than three years I prayed for God to take me home. Instead, He sent me a grandchild, a super special grandson that brought a new will to live. Though I was unable to work because of a compromised immune system and other issues I had to put together a new life, an entirely new life. I had not been completely successful in acquiring enough wealth to enter a stable retirement but my mental faculties sharpened up enough to make a few wise investment decisions, hopefully enough for retirement stability. So where was God in all this? I am convinced beyond a shadow of doubt that the whole disease thing was from God. Yes, an incurable disease sent my way by God himself.

The disease, my grandson, the care shown me by my wife and daughter all seemed to fit a plan. This plan generally took me out of public circulation. I was able to study scripture more during this time. And I had all day to devote to prayer should I feel I should. To be fully truthful, no, I never engaged in prayer all day. But I did learn how to be in prayer during this time. I stopped asking for healing early on. I had read enough scripture to see Bible figures testify of hearing from God. I never heard an audible voice but I do feel that God spoke to me in terms I can understand, His supreme mind to that small mind within His creation, me. I think all He wanted from me was for me to listen and act on His inaudible voice. He gave me tasks to do that I was capable of to keep me at least engaged in life. A new friend would present during this time too, a godly man that has been an enormous help to me.

God was finished with me in the business world. He had another calling for me. He gave me the opportunity to be a grandfather, a calling I have concentrated on mightily since even before my grandson was born. I believe I'm a pretty good grandpa to my very unique grandson. Most everything I do involves some consideration for him. Of course, sometimes I overdo it but I believe that to be a readily forgivable transgression. My life the last ten years, including the pain and suffering during acute phases of the disease, have been the best years of my life. I lost my keen analytical ability and the ability to field the facts and make an almost instant decision. But my relationship with God is much, much closer as I have, looking back, seen how He has used all this hardship, life threatening hardship for the good of my family, for me and for His kingdom.

There are many elements of the last fifteen years of my life that have brought pain and suffering, the greatest of which was the loss of my son. But even that considered, God used his death for many good things. My son's stated ambition in life was to make a difference. And he did make a difference, both good and bad. He made a profound difference in me. He was by no means a neutral influence on the world. His death absolutely crushed the family. The pain, as some that will read this know, is permanent. Admittedly, it lessens as time goes on but it is life enduring. The farther from his death I go the nearer I get to reunion. It has changed my life and most of all it changed my heart! The mind had a lot to sort through all while the heart was soaking it in. And through it all, even the death of my son, my faith grew stronger because God was with me. He was with me in His scripture, talking with me in prayer and teaching me what He wanted me to know. And He's with me this instant. I know it in my mind, feel it in my heart, and my soul is prepared to meet Him even now.

It has taken all my life for me to see and recognize God's influence and presence in my life. It's not very easy to see Denali up close and personal. The enormity is just overwhelming. Sometimes it is obscured in cloud cover. But from a distance, over time, from a variety of vantage points, watching and listening, studying and praying, through obedience and love, you can clearly see God's work in your life just as I did in mine. It's as plain as seeing God's work in creation. I cannot point to a single thing in my life that God didn't use for good, even the death of my son. And I love Him for His place in my life and for the redemption afforded me by His Son. It's where the heart and mind meet, delivering the soul to God, at the cross.

"Likewise the Spirit also helpeth our infirmities: for: we know not what we should pray for as we ought: but: the Spirit itself maketh intercession for us with groanings which cannot be uttered.. And he that searcheth the hearts knoweth what is the mind of the Spirit, because he maketh intercession for the saints according to the will of God. And we know that all things work together for good to them that love God, to them who are the called according to his purpose."

Romans 8:26-28 KJV

Chapter 7

With All My Heart

What do we think about the mind and its involvement in our faith, in our belief? I've heard many times that you can't think, you can't rationalize your relationship with God. God's ways are immeasurably higher than ours so, yes, in trying to figure out God I would surrender to the thought that we can never totally figure God out. But does that mean we shouldn't try to understand God more? Does it mean that the mind has no place in our faith? Is it like the separation of church and state, separation of the mind and soul? I would submit that we are all three as created human beings. Without the mind we do not function as God intended us to. My wife says I overanalyze everything. I'm pretty sure she is embellishing a bit but not entirely. I don't just want to know the answer. I want to know how the answer is arrived at. I want to know why. Why God does things is important in knowing God more, knowing God better. That God can never be fully known and understood just means we can engage in knowing and understanding more about Him all the time, as long as we live, thus, the need for continual study.

Can one be saved without thinking about it? Is salvation attainable without the mind evaluating the work of Jesus, the sinful nature of man and the registering of guilt necessary to sense the need for repentance? It might just be me, but I require thought to reach decisions, even quick knee-jerk decisions like those necessary to avoid calamity. I am just speaking from my own experience but I have had to think through lots of things in my life for many different reasons. Where God and His plan for my life are concerned, I really never gave much thought to how things in my life have been held within God's plan. I think I was taught not to look for answers on events, to just trust God basically blindly. I believe that leaves our relationship with God lacking a great deal. I believe that relegates our relationship with God to emotion alone. And we are so much more than emotion alone. We sense things like touch, sight, smell, sensation, pain and pleasure. We are capable of reasoning and learning, even offering theories on those things that may as yet be unproven. There are a lot of things that make up the human being, our ability to emote being only one. We liken emotion to the heart very often.

"Come now, and let us reason together, saith the LORD: though your sins be as scarlet, they shall be as white as snow; though they be red like crimson, they shall be as wool." Isaiah 1:18 KJV

Emotion, it has figured prominently in many bad decisions. I believe emotion is the link between the heart and the soul and is a catalyst for action on the part of the mind. Without thought, without contemplation by the mind we are left to emotion alone to sustain faith and our belief in God, the Holy Spirit, and even Jesus. I suppose I'm making an argument of an apologist in that we should be able to defend what we believe, even when the audience is just in the mirror. Admittedly, my defense of things involving faith is weak on many fronts. So I will think, I will use my mind immersed in scripture and prayer, to build up my ability to defend those things that I believe. I don't do that with sufficient frequency but I try to.

Sometimes emotion just takes over without sufficient action on the part of the mind. It's the physical, or more to the point the pleasurable, that overrules the common sense normally exerted by the mind. Irritation of various sorts often elicits a sudden flow of anger and sometimes even violence. When I was in high school a lifelong friend had been initiated into the sports club for varsity students one day. He was dumped in a nearby lake several times during the day of initiation. I learned of it in time to pester him about it while riding home on the school bus. Seated just behind him on the bus, noticing the sand in his hair, just as the bus was leaving school, I said to him, "nice day for a swim". It seemed with no thought at all he turned and smacked me in one fluid instantaneous motion. It was good for me. I'd say it was pretty good for him too. We were friends before, during and after that incident. We remain lifelong friends, close personal friends to this day. In retrospect, maybe it was not a good day for a swim after all. It was certainly not a good day for asking about it I assure you. But it was an emotional act that we both laugh about from time to time, obviously funnier to him than to me.

"He that is slow to anger is better than the mighty; and he that ruleth his spirit than he that taketh a city." Proverbs 16:32 KJV

"Let all bitterness, and wrath, and anger, and clamor, and evil speaking, be put away from you, with all malice: And be ye kind one to another, tenderhearted, forgiving one another, even as God for Christ's sake hath forgiven you."
Ephesians 4:31-32

Obviously, that first sight view of my wife was purely a matter of physical attraction, even in black and white, but I suspected there was more. I would have to examine the evidence and think about it. My mind would have to work on justifying the emotion, particularly in the mirror of my life. The emotional attachment was powerful because she was much more in person than a two dimensional black and white newsprint image. To make that attachment soul deep, to solidify a meaningful relationship, to understand what there was to her aside from her exceptional good looks required much thought and examination. There was careful consideration by both of us to mindfully justify the emotional attractions we shared. Much thought was involved by what would be the Wright family that followed. The mind was instrumental in facilitating that union. In fact, it was vital to our sustained relationship. I think that works the same way in our relationship with God.

The emotional attraction was made stronger by all I learned about my wife as we built our relationship. The physical attraction was strong from the very beginning and has not abated at all after forty five years. I once wondered, when we had only been married for a short time, how people still felt an attraction for their spouse when age set in. When I was in my twenties people in their fifties looked kind of old. People in their sixties were old and those older just didn't seem to be desirable anymore. Well I am in my sixties now, a young sixty six years, and I can say that I just don't see her through the eye of age. And I know she has aged. She's got all the rings, necklaces and bracelets of forty five years of marriage to prove it. When we talk I see her as she was when we first met. I see her more knowledgeable now. Her mind has worked on her through the years as has my mind worked on me. And we've worked on each other to come to general, maybe even specific, agreement on just about everything. We disagree on inconsequential stuff like my affection and self perceived need of sweets. But in the truly important things, those that test a life-long relationship, we are in lockstep.

I had to understand her and she me for things to last as long as they have. We've been through so much together. We brought two kids into the world, a daughter and a son. Our daughter lives next door with her husband Andy and our one and only grandson, Armour. We raised our kids to respect authority and to go by the rules. They didn't always do that nor did we. We went through hard times financially. We went through a period of separation resulting from poor life choices on my part. We went through a period of successful counseling to help restore our marriage. We accommodated demanding professional lives and full schedules. Incurable disease struck me sometime between 2007 and 2010. It took about three years to diagnose while my symptoms continued all but continuously. And if all that were not enough, coming out of nowhere, our son was killed instantly.

Sure, we all want to go to heaven. No? If you really don't want to go to heaven you might really want to concentrate on why. Maybe your emotions are in the way. Or, in the alternative, maybe your mind is in the way. Going to heaven is almost a no brainer requiring little thought. The objection seems to come into play when we are expected to believe certain things as a prerequisite to passing through the pearly gates. You can want to go to heaven and still not believe in Jesus, his birth, death or resurrection. I want to go to the moon someday. But that is more likely to happen than going to heaven in absence of the repentant belief in Christ as Savior. But you can still want to go, emotionally wish for inclusion in the heavenly realm, and even convince yourself that you are going to go. But emotion alone will not get you there. Christ is both the end and the means. Heaven is just the place He went to prepare for me. It is where I will live. It is where my reward, optimal for me, will be. It's where my son is presently. My mind has concluded that heaven is the place for me to be. My mind concluded that Jesus was the Way, the only Way. But going to heaven is not actually a decision. Trusting in and following Christ is. The decision on heaven is one Jesus made for those that believe. If you believe, then Heaven is afforded you by the work Jesus did on the cross. It's not a decision you or I can make, just going to heaven.

Once I reached that decision, the decision to accept Jesus as my personal Savior, then the work was complete. He did all the work! So for many years thereafter, having concluded the decision to follow Christ, I largely abandoned the actual walk. Other pursuits claimed my attention. I worked pretty hard at fishing and hunting and preparing for a job after school. I spent much time in pursuit of the one who would share my life and would welcome me into her life. Parenthetically, I must admit, just as a friend noted not long ago, that I kicked way out of my field of coverage in this pursuit. And after school I spent nearly all my waking hours in career pursuits in an area of the country not known for tall ladders to climb. And it was during the years after the Carter presidency so I had to work all the harder. My employer was quite fair with me and allowed me to do things that would not have normally been available to me until I had years and years of experience.

We went to church where Denise grew up, forty miles away in Clarkrange, Tennessee. Her church was a Methodist congregation of God fearing families, very traditional, soundly led by a pastor displaying a call. Other than the order of service it was not very different from the southern Baptist church I grew up in eighteen miles to the north. Those we went to church with lived their faith and the appearance was that of a one mind congregation, a house undivided as it appeared, was in practice. After our daughter was born we decided to select a church where we lived and moved our membership accordingly. I miss that period because Sundays were largely all day. Most businesses were closed on Sunday and family took center stage when services ended. We retired to her grandparents' home for Sunday dinner with family. Visiting with the extended family was facilitated by her grandparents, Mr. and Mrs. Martin. Mr. Martin sang tenor in the choir and Mrs. Martin played the organ. If ever there were examples of Christians living the sold out to Christ life every day, it was the Martins.

But I was saved, right? I had made the right decision! I had checked all the boxes. Bound for heaven! So now I could channel my life efforts in other directions, more important directions or so I thought. I mean, that's what it's all about isn't it? And it was clearly not just an emotional decision but one that I had examined the evidence, thought it through, reached a decision and acted on it. Full stop! So life went on for twenty years or so until I had to face the inevitable loss of my father to cancer. Cracks started appearing in the family of my childhood. My dad had cancer and my mother had been diagnosed with rheumatoid arthritis. At this point in my life I had no clue that my immune system was like my baldness, inherited from my mother's side of the family.

My dad and I were very close. We agreed on most everything from politics to finances, religion and faith, and living life with at least a little programmed recreation such as annual vacations at the beach, hunting together on Thanksgiving morning and fishing at the pond on the farm. On a drive from my home to his one Saturday morning, along about the road that leads to Little Crab, not audible but more powerful, I sensed a message that my father would soon die and I would face the rest of my life without him. And I would be able to handle it. He would help me. It was like being divinely prepared for the loss and the things that would be required of me in the years after his death. I was given a time, in fact nearly two years, to become prepared for his death. He was eighty two when he died and his mind had not dimmed. His mind was sharper at eight two than mine is at sixty six. He was quite analytical though not very mechanical. He examined scripture all his life and applied his mind to the pursuit of wanting to know God better. I get it! It was a decision, mindfully considered, and one he privately pursued. Only until he was approaching death did dad and I ever discuss those things of everlasting importance.

So after accepting Christ at the age of nine, until my father died when I was in my forties, exercising my faith if you can call it exercising, was just church attendance with an ear toward hearing the last amen on Sunday. As I believe is true with so many Christians today, I was going to heaven and that's all I really needed to know. What a pitiful state of faith. The loss of my dad brought the first questions, the need to know, of what happens when we die. So I read the Bible through for the first time. I still have that Bible and it shows the wear. I took it on business trips. It accompanied me hunting. I read much of it sitting in a tree stand and in an airliner. Many are the afternoons I looked up from it to discover a herd of deer just under my feet. And I read books about heaven, mostly the celebrated been there and back books. And most of my questions were satisfied over the few years after his death. I was certain I would see dad again and that he persisted in life even the instant after death. I knew he would soon die and die he did.

But the more I studied, the more I was presented with things I needed to know. Eschatology became a favorite topic of study. For real, I would probably be alive when Christ returns and I needed to know precisely what would happen and when it would unfold. I've read thousands of pages, volume after volume of works on end times. And for better than forty years I had it all worked out, got it completely, I knew everything but the day Jesus would return. Oh, I couldn't defend it and I filled the holes in with out of context, misinterpreted scripture but I was convinced I understood it completely. And then a few years ago my inability to defend my eschatological beliefs was cause to revisit the study. And since, I have changed my views to a position I can defend, one I feel is scripturally sound, satisfied to the point I no longer feel the need to study end times.

And what did I conclude? It would be a book all by itself so suffice it to say that the conclusions that matter in my life would center in the thought that end times, the final events, would likely not be for me to face in this body. Every time I hear a religious figure, claiming of a troubling headline that Jesus is on His way, I am convinced that they have no clue when He will return. In fact, scripture reveals that His return will be a surprise, as a thief comes in the night. So I'm unconcerned about the very end. Indeed, I do expect to die first and return with Christ when He does come back.

So it is that it's with all my heart that I believe Jesus came, lived a perfect life, surrendered His life on the cross to a save a sinner, even and particularly, to save me if no other. And He did it with calculation. My heart is all in! And it took my mind to wrap my heart around that. And that's what I'm offering with this book. My growing experience, the relationship built and growing with a loving God, took on an urgency unlike any I ever felt after the tragic loss of my son thirteen years ago. So this book, these lines and words, are about my journey in loving God with all my mind. It is the record from me to you of the issues and problems I mindfully considered during the relationship building phase of my life and just why it's important to engage the heart, mind and soul in the pursuit of knowing God, knowing God better and better.

"But seek ye first the kingdom of God, and his righteousness; and all these things shall be added unto you."
Matthew 6:33 KJV

Study God's word prayerfully to know God better and better and better and better.

Chapter 8

Images

I was looking at a few pictures my wife posted on social media a few days ago. I noticed a familiar feeling on an unexpected subject in the pictures. As I examined the pictures I remembered how the person looked when here, still living. Patience and contentment came to mind as I looked at the subject. The memories struck were so familiar to me, cherished images of times past. Though at home alone, I just had to smile and laugh out loud a little as I gazed at the collection of just a few photographs. The images of the subjects are all that remain.

Occasionally I see a photo of my grandfather Porter Mullinix. He died in 1955, three years before I was born. It seems like I remember him quite well, but how could I? I was told stories about grandpa Mullinix early in life continuing up until there was no one left alive to tell them. Every little bit of passing time I would hear another story about him. He was quite the comical actor in life. In the family he is a bit of a legend, at least to me. I've always thought I would like to be just like him. I could do without the notorious forgetfulness even though I'm experiencing it myself now, but I do covet his reputed dry humor. He tended to look off a good bit when driving a car. I catch myself doing that far too much. Maybe we all do that. I guess he just wasn't made to stay here forever. But every time I see his image, even when I think of him without being reminded by something, pleasant feelings flood my mind. I love him in absentia having never heard his voice or seen him pink and above ground.

My grandmother Wright is another one that is fondly remembered. I see her picture far too seldom. She had eight girls and three boys. She buried a son named Casto when he was a child and a son named Carl when he was a young adult. Carl was killed in a car wreck in view of grandma's home when he was just twenty two years old. Grandma lived well into old age and was the calendar picture grandmother. She had a wonderfully simple sense of humor. Her preferred wardrobe never, never ever changed from my earliest memory of her until her death. One photograph looked just like the next. If I remember anything about her I remember her statement as she would get up from her rocker and head to her bedroom. As she rose she would say, "My head's just a bustin'!" Her adult children had the habit of talking all at the same time and with every decibel they could muster. Your head would "just be a bustin'" too if exposed for a very long time to the rapid fire syllables and sheer volume, stamina too. The content and speed of the voices would be testy sometimes too. She was a small woman but a strong woman. She was a woman of conviction and faith. She referred to God as, "The Good Lord".

My grandmother Mullinix died when I was a small child and I have no memory of her. I see her picture and have to be reminded that it is granny's image otherwise I wouldn't recognize her at all. I probably know less about granny Mullinix than any of my close ancestors. She lost children to death too. I suppose the thing that comes to mind when I see her image is of the death of her daughter, Bulah, of unknown causes. My mother wrote about her death, how granny, in the spring of the year, would bring the box containing her long lost daughter's belongings outside to air. As she sat near the box of things she would cry and cry. So pity and deep compassion register, melting the hardness of my mind. I know all too well that feeling that was the source of granny's sorrow.

I have a hard time looking at a picture of my parents without looking at them both at the same time. They were quite different. I suppose if opposites attract that would explain a good many things. Dad was very analytical yet not very mechanical. Mom was the artsy parent and was far more patient that dad. So when I see them in a picture together I see everything to be desired in a parent, just not all of them resident in either one. But together my parents were the total package. My siblings might take exception to my assessment but still it is the way I view them. They tried in different ways to steer their children in the right direction. I think they did their best. They both were strong in their faith. But it is really dad that makes me look at them together as an entity.

Mom lived long enough to have two lives. Dad died just a few days into 2002 and she lived until September 2014. The last word from his mouth was "Blanche". So now I do look at her separately from dad. She developed a whole other life during the twelve years following his death. She moved to be nearer two of her middle aged kids. In fact, she lived just a few miles from me. I would stop by often to check on her and visit. I never caught her doing just nothing. She would be reading, playing the organ, painting or studying the Bible. Painting was a special love of hers and she was quite good at it. All of her kids kept a couple of her paintings. As she lived on I thought mother was a bit gullible and lacked the skill to navigate life on her own. But as I look at her image on paper now I realize that she was quite able and anything but gullible. She handled family issues very differently than I would have but her way worked for her and it worked for the family. She was a force of class too. If she ever left the house less than dressed to kill it would've been an urgent matter of life and death. No, when she went out, her hair was "fixed", she was dressed appropriately and would have fit in at a formal event or a church dinner equally well. I have learned most from her looking at her image. Though she went ahead ten years ago she is still very present in my life. I married one just like her.

And my son Alex, I look at his image most often, never a day missing at least a brief look. His image is the screensaver on my phone and my iPad. It's the background on my wristwatch. Unlike the aforementioned family members, I have many images of Alex. Do you ever look at images of those gone ahead and remember things you did years ago? I do that with some images but not images of Alex. And that's not because there were few memories to recall. As a matter a fact they would be almost limitless. But when I see his image the first thing in my mind is how long he will have to wait before we are there with him. I think of the first things that will happen in his presence when I get there myself. I imagine those things we will do in the place Jesus went to prepare for us. There is no dread when I see his image, just deep longing and an eagerness for expedience.

But when viewing this first image, the image on my wife's post on social media, I didn't even realize at first that he's not gone just yet. He is still very much with us living as large as he can. It is as if I remembered how the person looked as if he was still here. The person, well, the person in her post, well, it was my image. I caught myself looking at images of myself in the same way I look at the images of my family members gone ahead, already dead, dead for years. And why is that? Why do I look at my image as if I'm already gone when I know quite well that I'm still living? I think it's likely that I look at these most recent images with almost a third person approval, with a knowledge that I'm finally what I was to be of most importance in life. I am settled in my faith, confident in my beliefs, satisfied with the end of the sixty sixth year of my life and a fair to middlin' grandpa to my only very special grandchild. I see in the image, one who was here, and is and will remain far from perfect, but one who is very conscious of the need to be better, to try. I am pleased with my image when I look at it as if I'm already gone. I have not always been able to look at my image and have a feeling of approval however modest it might be. I hope that's an indication that my family will view it the same way when I have gone ahead. Maybe they will smile and laugh a little.

And as I write I remember the things that now seem so distant and disconnected from those social media images posted by Denise. The person that was wrapped up in the job, the person that answered cell phone calls anytime and all the time, the person that put the family somewhere on down the list of importance just seems so foreign to the present image. I like my present image better than those of the first fifty five years. And I wonder, after I've gone ahead, will the remaining family tell my grandson Armour those things that Pa did the fifty years before his birth? Will he care to know that I patented the first titanium football facemask? Will he care that as a defense contractor my ABVM score was 100? Even I don't care about that! It just doesn't matter now. Maybe it's not even a good thing. It's more important that what I was to Armour was what I was supposed to be. It is far more important that he see my resolute faith in God than it is to see my ability to process numbers. That I cared for him and my daughter and wife more than anything else earthly is what needs to come to mind as he grows and occasionally sees my image.

That he and I grew birdhouse gourds and made birdhouses out of them, following our feathered friends as they resided in our work, that's what my image should call up. That he and I spun and bottled honey with his name leading my family title on the label, Armour and Pa's Honey Ranch, that image definitely will carry. Discovering wildflowers together, catching and releasing problem raccoons, fishing in a friend's pond, for sure the first fish he caught all need to flood his memory when he sees my image. That he was important from birth in his grandpa's eyes, that's what I hope he sees. The value of creation divinely spoken into being, God's watch over of us, the importance and vitality and truth of the Bible and the salvation available to him through, and only through, a penitent, real relationship with Christ, that should be the standard he sees when he views my image.

And I hope my daughter sees every bit as much when she comes upon my image. I don't treat her quite as well as I do my grandson. I know that sounds awful but it's true. I had a different role to live with my kids than I have with my only grandson. With the kids discipline was shared by my wife and me. We saw right and wrong identically. We didn't always agree on everything but we seldom disagreed on discipline. I felt my job as a parent was to try to guide my kids to successful adulthood. That's a very different role than being grandpa. I think my daughter needed my support and encouragement and I feel I delivered it the best way I knew how. Now in my sixties I would probably make a few decisions differently. But I didn't have the luxury of raising kids forty years after their birth. Together with her mother, I tried to guide her steps in life critically. That was easy. She made very good decisions, stayed focused and worked hard to reach her goals. She works hard still and I believe that was instilled at home as she grew up. But I hope, as she is now a parent herself that she sees the role of a parent is not nearly as glamorous as is the role of grandpa. Maybe Armour will deliver her a grandchild in his own image, which is very much in her image. She should be so fortunate. If she doesn't understand me now, she will then.

And I enjoy looking at my wife's image. When I see her image I see physical beauty and determination. I see a woman, heels dug in, with her hands on the hood of the hearse coming to get me, straining against its forward motion with all her knowledge, ability and strength. She's held the hearse at bay for well over a decade with her watch over me and care for me when I'm sick. She understands all the afflictions that inhabit my aging, diseased body and every decision seems as if they are all calculated in the result. We are not too far apart in age. It's the mileage, you see, that makes the difference. I see her patience with most people and a willingness to help others. I see unwavering adherence to rules and the way things should be. I envy that. There was a time I was more concerned with the rules and the way things should be but now I am more focused on what everlasting life holds for both of us. I see a person that will be able to look at her own image and say to the mirror when the hearse reaches its destination, "I did everything I could." I wonder what thoughts my image will elicit in her when I have finally gone on ahead.

Just a few weeks ago my image was a little fuzzy. It had been fuzzy in my view for years. It took writing my book "Will I Have Wings?" to bring the image into focus. It's important that our images, yours and mine, reflect Christ in our lives. If Christ was a little dim in my life before writing that book, it had to be coming through forcefully with my unapologetic written position of Christ in my life. And I believe that's why I see a different image when I look at my image now. It's an image that reminds me where and when I yielded to God's will for my life. And it was anything but easy. Anyone that has read the book knows it had to be gut wrenching to write. It brought darkness to the family for a few weeks. My wife and daughter read it before it was published. It would never be a book they would read voluntarily. It is unlikely they will ever read it again. Oh, they might read it were it factual events of some celebrity. But it's not. The events are deeply personal to the family and bring much pain freshly to mind.

I am always fascinated with the images we have available for Christ. Of course, that I know of, there are no actual artist renderings that Jesus sat for when He walked the earth. All of them are artists' representations of what comes to their minds as they apply paint to canvas. It is unlikely that any of them are spot on. I've seen images of Jesus with both long hair and short hair. If I was created in His image He was bald and a little too heavy. I've seen images of a pearly white Jesus and also as a person of color. For some reason I look right passed the color of His skin and his head of hair and body of health. But I see a lot when I look at any depiction of Christ's image.

I see the Jesus present at creation. The first chapter of the Gospel according to John confirms that. I see God. I see God in human form. I see sacrifice. I see the Sacrifice. I see the Sacrifice paying for, enabling my everlasting life. I see forty days of temptation in the wilderness. I see water turned into wine. I see a few fish miraculously multiplied feeding thousands and thousands. I see the blind granted sight, the lame given use of their legs, the sick healed. I see the demon possessed liberated. I see the mere touch of the hem of His garment shooting divine power throughout the body of the faithful reach. I see a man walking on water, commanding storms to cease. I see the elements brought to submission by His mere spoken word so to do. I see reconciliation, reconciliation of the world to God by the Way, the only Way by which it could be reconciled. I see quite a lot in an instant when I see Jesus, even a mental picture of Him.

"In the beginning was the Word, and the Word was with God, and the Word was God. The same was in the beginning with God. All things were made by him; and without him was not any thing made that was made. In him was life; and the life was the light of men. And the light shineth in darkness; and the darkness comprehended it not. There was a man sent from God, whose name was John. The same came for a witness, to bear witness of the Light, that all men through him might believe. He was not that Light, but was sent to bear witness of that Light. That was the true Light, which lighteth every man that cometh into the world. He was in the world, and the world was made by him, and the world knew him not. He came unto his own, and his own received him not. But as many as received him, to them gave he power to become the sons of God, even to them that believe on his name: Which were born, not of blood, nor of the will of the flesh, nor of the will of man, but of

God. And the Word was made flesh, and dwelt among us, (and we beheld his glory, the glory as of the only begotten of the Father,) full of grace and truth."
  John 1:1-14 KJV

Born the Son of God to a virgin, the coming of Jesus was foretold hundreds of years earlier. I see a star marking the place of his humble birth. I see kings bringing gifts to the King, the Royal Infant of eternal Divinity. I see the Father's watchful protection over His only Son. I see Jesus teaching. I see Jesus calling His disciples to go out and spread the good news. I see Him in the synagogue teaching and outside turning the tables on the moneychangers. I see Him raising the dead. That reads a little too easy. Read again! I see Him raising the dead! I see Him! I see Christ, not exactly His precise physical image. But I see all those things that He was, is and ever shall be.

I see Him betrayed, beaten to a pulp, thorns thrust into his head, bleeding. I see Him restrained from calling destruction on the earth because of His love of the world, because of His love for me. I see Him insulted, His garments divided by lot. I see Him impaled with a spear, a sudden flow of redeeming blood expelled from the body of the Savior and in so doing, completing the work required to save me. I see Him crucified. I see Him crucified! I! See! Him! Killed! I see a risen Savior that would ascend to Heaven in clear view. There are so many images that form a mental deluge of instant recognition of what Christ is to me, to the world. They are all real. I expect that I have no false image of Christ though some would deny Him. All those things that have come to mind when I see His image are documented. They are true. They were witnessed and recorded for the memory of the world. The Bible tells me so.

"An when he had spoken these things, while they beheld, he was taken up; and a cloud received him out of their sight. And while they looked stedfastly toward heaven as he went up, behold, two men stood by them in white apparel; Which also said, Ye men of Galilee, why stand ye gazing up into heaven?

this same Jesus, which is taken up from you into heaven, shall so come in like manner as ye have seen him go into heaven." Acts 1:9-10 KJV

But I also see with these rapid recollections the more personal things that are Him. I see Him coming to earth, living a sinless life. I see Him asking the Father, if it is in His will to let the cup of death, the penalty for my sins, pass from Him. And I see Him paying the price for me. I see Him going through all that so that I might have life everlasting. Might, I ask myself? It's actually a certainty with a penitent belief in Christ as Savior and Redeemer. I see He has a plan for me. I see He has words for me to hear and actions for me to take. I see Him listening to me. I see Him holding my son. I see Him holding me. I see Him alive! I see Him returning. I see Him!

I surely see a lot when I look at the image of Jesus yet it doesn't just fill my mind with all He is. Contemplating Jesus, seeing Jesus, listening for and to Jesus, and talking with Jesus all build this recognition of all that He is in an instant. And I believe knowing Him, having a deeply personal relationship with Him, establishes the instant spiritual flood of all that He is to me in a building crescendo that consumes more and more of my time as I seek to be nearer and nearer to Him. That moment of realizing all those things at once becomes, should become, and will become more and more of one's life. He is what we should be all about. See Him? Can you see Him? Are you looking for Him? See His image in your life. His image should come through, should be reflected by your life. I look for it in my own. And sometimes I see it, though not nearly enough.

But what do I see when I view the image of the unseen God, the God of the Old Testament? I have seen painted images of an artist's thoughts of what God the Father might appear as, his image. The power on display by God is so immense as to totally escape estimation. "Let there be light", and so there was light. The image of creation in the description we have from Genesis might be considered the stuff of fairy tales by some but the physical image of creation itself sustains every word of it. He made it all. And He made all things work together in an order that has been maintained for thousands of years. I see his work in the colonies of honey bees, how they work in concert, in their pollination of the plants that provide all we eat and that is pleasurable to the eye. And from space one can see His work with the earth and moon and stars, set in motion during creation and still in motion yet today. I see His plan for us, His love for the earth and His creation, especially those created in His image. Most of all I see the Father giving of His Son, His very life, as a sacrifice for me.

And still today I see a member of the triune God still here, still with me, as close, as close as anyone can be, even inside those that have placed their trust in Christ, inside me. His image is most difficult to see. It's in our actions He can be most clearly seen. How we respond to His constant counsel shows how clearly we see His image. Some might see Him as the angel on a shoulder. I must admit I do not. I see Him as integral to my being. If I am to listen and follow where He directs, then He must be on both shoulders. He doesn't always give me the answer I prefer but I'm never internally without the proper argument. And He gives a nod now and then in approval or disapproval of my actions before God. He's real. He's here. And I need Him!

The image of the Godhead reveals all of Him, the Father, the Son and the Holy Ghost. It has taken me a long time to clear up these images, much longer than it should have. It should be the compelling force in one's life, the force that turns an insatiable desire to know God into the action of having that relationship that bursts with a growing familiarity of the image of God, a spiritual clarity that yields the true image of God, an image reflected in one's own image as seen by others, Christ in my life.

"And there are also many other things which Jesus did, the which if they should be written every one, I suppose that even the world itself would not contain the books that should be written."
John 21:25 KJV

Chapter 9

Thinking Jesus Through

Jesus is not really hard to figure out. One might suggest that Jesus was the most perfect work of God in creation. Wait a minute, unlike you and me Jesus was not created. Co-equal with God, indeed God himself, Jesus was not created nor was he made by God. As is true with God the Father, Jesus always was. He was, is and is to come. That Jesus was born into our world makes it hard for us to know Him truly as He was, is and will be when again we see him. He will come again. It would seem we make him co-equal with us instead of co-equal with God. That's a good starting place to get to know Jesus and understand His ability to save us, to save me, from my sins.

As a human being, one hundred percent human while being one hundred percent God, Jesus did things on earth that no human being did before Jesus was born or since He was born. Jesus was the only one to walk the face of the earth that was the Son of God. Jesus was not created as was the first human being, Adam. Jesus came to earth for one reason, to display God's love for mankind, to be the one and only suitable sacrifice to save mankind from sin. It was the only Way. It was not God punting for a failed part of his creation. No, it was God's plan and the supreme show of love planned from the very beginning. God, being omniscient, knew mankind would fail with his God given free will. There was no doubt in God's mind. If there's one thing God is likely incapable of it is doubt. Surprise is very likely foreign to God as a simple matter of His omniscience.

No other man entered life on earth through the birth of a virgin. There are those that question whether that is actually true. In Jesus' time the king took Jesus the infant as a real threat. The threat was not that Jesus was known to be born of a virgin. He was to be the King of the Jews. I suppose one wouldn't have to claim virgin birth for a king of that time to sense a threat. Jesus birth was singular in history with all the angelic announcements and displays that the gospels speak to us about. Many infants lost their lives as the king sought to find and kill the infant Jesus. Mary and Joseph fled to Egypt taking Jesus with them. No human being was ever born this way. There have been other accounts of virgin births, doubtful in my mind, but none preceded by the angelic displays announcing the coming birth of Jesus, God incarnate.

It would seem Jesus fit in well as a child and an adolescent from all I can tell from scripture. But it's when He started acting like God that things started to come to question. We have many walking the earth today that claim to possess supernatural powers. Quite frankly, I have my doubts. One thing I know for certain is that no man possesses supernatural power by one's own means. But Jesus started doing things that really attracted attention. He was healing blindness, making the lame walk again and even raising people from the dead. He was casting out demons, walking on water, multiplying a sparse amount of food to feed thousands on more than one occasion. But He was also a carpenter. He was the most extraordinary human ever to live and the only One who could truthfully say that if you had seen Him you had seen the Father. That is Jesus. He wasn't just acting like God. He was, is and continues to be God, a member of the triune God.

Jesus was the answer to prophecies recorded by multiple writers hundreds of years before His birth. His virgin birth was foretold. His divinity was foretold. Even His death on the cross was foretold long, long before the man Jesus ever entered the world in human form. The long awaited Savior of the world was finally here, on earth, preparing to sacrifice Himself for the world, for me, too, as if for no other. His entire human life was purposed to sacrifice His life for the lives of those He loved. Blood sacrifice as prescribed in scripture had been practiced for thousands of years. Jesus would give His own blood to meet the need for once and final payment, sufficient to save the world, atonement for all those who repent and believe in Him. No further blood sacrifice would be required, His being perfectly sufficient, a fully complete, never ending atonement.

This is just me thinking, but how could the shed blood of a lamb cover the sins of a human being? Certainly, I would not suggest that the blood of a lamb equals the value of a human being or the cost of a person's sin. A lamb was just simply not a like kind considered sufficient for the salvation of the whole world. And as is true of human beings, no lamb has yet to be found perfect, totally and absolutely without blemish. Rest assured, you might not see it, but there is a flaw somewhere. The offering is less than sufficient. The act of sacrifice was prescribed in the Old Testament but it was anything but complete. And as a result, it had to be repeated over and over and over and over. I really believe that God used the act of blood sacrifice for several things, one being to show how futile and incomplete it really was. The world would need a Savior, One worthy to save all that would call on His name. And all the goats and sheep that ever lived could not save a lost and dying world.

So it would take a like kind to be sufficient to pay for the sins of the world. But to provide a complete and durable atonement the sacrifice must be without blemish, totally and absolutely without blemish. No one else in history can lay claim to the qualification of Savior of the world but Jesus, the Son of God. Jesus lived a life totally without sin. And it was not that He was without temptation. Jesus withstood temptation so great that I just cannot imagine it. Still, Jesus did not sin. And unlike all that have ever lived, I believe that He withstood temptation by human strength. He was indeed one of us while being God incarnate. Jesus singularly met the like kind, without blemish, indeed perfect requirements to once and for all provide the sacrifice of Himself for those that would accept His payment for their sins, for mine. One, and only One, sacrifice met the sufficiency to pay for all the sins of the world, past, present and future.

"Then was Jesus led up of the Spirit into the wilderness to be tempted of the devil. And when he had fasted forty days and forty nights, he was afterward an hungered. And when the tempter came to him, he said, If thou be the Son of God, command that these stones be made bread. But he answered and said, It is written, Man shall not live by bread alone, but by every word that proceedeth out of the mouth of God. Then the devil taketh him up into the holy city, and setteth him on a pinnacle of the temple, And saith unto him, If thou be the Son of God, cast thyself down: for it is written, He shall give his angels charge concerning thee: and in their hands they shall bear thee up, lest at any time thou dash thy foot against a stone. Jesus said unto him, It is written again, Thou shalt not tempt the Lord thy God. Again, the devil taketh him up into an exceeding high mountain, and sheweth him all the kingdoms of the world, and the glory of them; And saith unto him, All these things will I give thee, if thou wilt fall down and worship me. Then saith Jesus unto him, Get thee hence, Satan: for it is written, Thou shalt worship the Lord thy God, and him only shalt thou serve. Then the devil leaveth him, and, behold, angels came and ministered unto him." Matthew 4:1-11 KJV

But sacrificing Himself was not all Jesus did while He walked the face of the earth. He gave important instruction on how one should live life. Chief among these instructions were displays of how he lived His brief life on earth. He studied, He taught and He ministered to both the rich and the poor. Jesus was criticized for being around those who were imperfect by those that just could not see their own imperfection, their own sin.

Jesus was actively ministering to the sick and the needy as well as the tax collectors. It would appear, and is in fact true, that Jesus loved all people. He practiced what He preached. It must have been difficult indeed for those that condemned Him to die on the cross to find fault in Him. And what was the fault they took such exception with? It was that Jesus had made claims privately, claims they considered blasphemous, of being God, of being the prophesied Messiah. For once in history, the only One before, since or after Who could innocently lay claim to actually being Divinity was sentenced to die on the cross for actually being what He claimed to be.

And what about the cross, how does it fit? I don't mean to tell the story of the cross. I expect those that will read this are just as familiar with the cross as am I, likely more so. If Jesus is who He claimed to be, could He not have used His power to destroy His enemies? I believe He could have. But no, Jesus willingly took His place to afford me with durable atonement for my sin. I believe Jesus' command of His faculties allowed Him to experience the sins of the world as if they were all His own. I believe He saw me, my image as he was suffering crucifixion. I believe He personally and humanly realized and experienced the punishment for every sin I would ever commit nearly two thousand years before I committed them. It was the ultimate act of His love for me, this author, as personal as if I were the only one He died for. That's worth understanding. You see, what Jesus did, sacrificing Himself to pay for a world of sin was deeply personal. He did it for me! He provided the payment for my sins. His sacrifice was all sufficient and durable into everlasting life. The quality of the sacrifice was absolutely infinite in coverage.

"For as much as ye know that ye were not redeemed with corruptible things, as silver and gold, from your vain conversation received by tradition from your fathers; But with the precious blood of Christ, as of a lamb without blemish and without spot: Who verily was foreordained before the

foundation of the world, but was manifest in these last times for you, Who by him do believe in God, that raised him up from the dead, and gave him glory; that your faith and hope might be in God." I Peter 1:18-21 KJV

So what has Jesus done for the world lately? As if He just spoke them this morning, His words still ring true today. I think of these words every single day. Jesus said that we should love God with all our heart, soul and mind and that we should love others as we love ourselves. Those commands seem to be quite broad when it comes to practice. Loving God is a lifelong growing process. I doubt the human mind and heart can ever gain total knowledge and understanding of God. But we can learn. Our minds can glean from scripture how God behaves in certain circumstances and just how perfect He is. A mind committed to learning more about God produces a heart that has an ever growing love for God resulting in a soul confident in His ability to hold us safe from eternal separation and torment. A better, closer walk with Jesus brings a life lacking a fear of death and a satisfaction with one's own life and confidence in the promise of everlasting life. By no means does that mean that our lives will be without difficulty. But it does mean that our everlasting life will be everything Heaven promises to be.

"For God so loved the world, that he gave his only begotten Son, that whosoever believeth in him should not perish, but have everlasting life." John 3:16. KJV

I can only share with you some of the things that I have practiced in my life to gain a better understanding of God, and of Jesus and of the Holy Spirit. I have looked for answers in life both through study of the Bible, listening to sound preaching and time in private prayer. But mostly I have asked for the Holy Spirit's guidance in getting to know God better. I feel the need to appreciate as much as humanly possible just what God has done for me. Beyond that, and this is the most difficult, I have tried to learn what God would have me do in the circumstances

I have faced. I find I can best learn that by reading and meditating on scripture. I don't skip any of it including the genealogies. I engage my mind in understanding why this God, invisible to me, would give His only Son to save me. I struggle to answer the question were the roles reversed. Thankfully I am not God or the world would be in real trouble.

Don't give up on God right after the walk up the aisle and the baptism. A growing faith is built over time. It is built in dedicated study of scripture and devotion to prayer. Indeed, most of my praise of God is during my private prayer time. We associate praise as belonging in the church setting and it certainly does. But that is by no means the only appropriate time to worship the Creator of all that is, the Savior of the world and my constant companion the Holy Spirit. I've said it over and over, the best worship service I was ever in, I was the only one there. Be a leader in your own personal worship. I don't read the Bible like a storybook or a novel. I believe with all my heart it is the God breathed owner's manual for mankind. That belief took much mindful study, prayer and application to engage the heart in a growing appreciation and faith in and love for God. And I'm not talking about just what He did for me. I'm also talking about the counsel available to me today. And further, I am also saying that He holds my soul, that part of me which is eternally durable, in His hands.

"For the which cause I also suffer these things: nevertheless I am not ashamed: for I know whom I have believed, and am persuaded that he is able to keep that which I have committed unto him against that day." II Timothy 1:12 KJV

There is no downside to engaging one's mind in the study of just how great God is. I have avoided most of the how-to books, daily Bible reading booklets and opinions of most others in favor of how God speaks to me every single day. The thought occurred to me long ago that people were being saved before most of the conveniences we have today. I am not condemning sources of study other than the Bible but one must take caution in selecting them and proving what they teach with scripture itself. Scripture actually admonishes us to do just that. That applies to the heard word too. Preachers are not infallible. I consider myself quite fortunate to be sitting under the preaching of a very reliable preacher at this time in my life. That hasn't always been true. Prove out what you read, hear and observe with scripture and prayer.

Some might suggest that I am making Christianity far too difficult. But to the contrary, it is incredibly easy to realize one's own sins and seek to find a solution. Jesus is that solution. I trust I have made the case. Trust in His ability to cover your sins, repent and be saved. That's no more difficult than it is. One's mind must still be engaged. It does require a bit of thought but it's not beyond the ability of mankind to understand the plan God laid out to redeem mankind from the curse of sin. It requires minimal thought but it does require thought. And thought provokes a yearning and a void in the heart that only Jesus can fill. What I am suggesting here is something a lot of professing Christians miss in there walk: a growing faith, comfort and trust in Christ, not just fire insurance. That takes desire and time, your desire and time. It takes up an increasing amount of my time to grow ever closer to the Master of the universe.

The loss of my Son and incurable illness brought more questions than this mind could answer on its own. I devoted hours and hours, day after day for years, looking for the answer to why healthy people die so young. Why do accidents take the innocent? Am I being punished? When will I die? Why have I contracted an incurable disease for which there is no explanation as to the cause? Why can I not receive healing this very minute? Or maybe I have. How would I know? What was happening to my son the moment after He died? Does he suffer still? Does he have a physical body now? Is he aware of his family left behind here on earth? Is he aware of others that died without Christ? Does he know about his nephew born three years after his death? Will he know me? Can he see what happens here on earth? Is he with my parents? Has he met Jesus face to Face? What does it feel like to be well and live forever?

All these questions I feel I have soundly answered in my mind, building a growing faith that only craves more of this Jesus. Seek out the truth! Seek out Jesus, the Way, the Truth and the Life.

Chapter 10

Heart, Soul and………MIND

Warm weather holiday weekends are all about camping, boating, cooking out and going on vacation, no? Well no! Memorial Day in particular is shrouded in pain and dipped in blood. And I think on things like what those that served and died left behind for us. I was never in the armed forces though it is beginning to look like that might be demanded of me sometime in the future. I'm just a grandpa, probably the most significant period of my sixty six years. "Best friends forever" were my grandson Armour's words yesterday as we loaded up the pickup to go fishing at the pond of a good friend. And that's what we are. But I have to be more. I must!

Sometimes inspiration comes from minor points in a message. It touches my heart. A couple of years ago I heard a brief couple of statements made by a man nearing fifty years of age. He briefly recounted how hard losing his grandpa was. It seems I remember he was in his teen years, maybe older though that's not important to the story. He was very close to his grandpa and the pain of the loss was still visible on his face and in his voice as he spoke. So is the pain what's important? Of course it's not. It is what's behind that pain that makes the difference for the good. He was heartbroken. So having heard these words and observed his face as he spoke, the message sank in just how important the role of grandpa is in touching the heart of a grandson.

It's easier for me I suppose. I have one grandchild and that's the eternal full plate of grandchildren for me. I'm cognizant of the influence I have on him but still some of the bad grandpa comes through. It is my hope that he takes away more good from me than bad. But I'm the responsible party in making certain I deliver more of one and less of the other and I will try. If it hurts him a little bit when I'm gone that's a good thing. If he remembers me fondly the rest of his life, well, until he sees me and Uncle Alex and great Uncle Terry again, that's a good thing too. But it's what he takes away into life and beyond death from Pa that counts. I hope it's good. I trust it will be. That's my service to the country aside from paying taxes. It's delivering a grandson to a loving relationship with God and responsible citizenship. And in that I believe that honors those that died for my privilege so to do.

As for the speaker recounting the story of the loss of his grandfather, he's a preacher now. He did well by his grandpa and his grandpa by him. That's the goal of this grandpa too. Maybe another grandpa will hear the same words one day about this grandpa. This speaker, well really a preacher though it's not exactly fashionable to refer to members of the clergy as preachers these days, is not one to burst into tears at every little thing. He is not afraid to display emotion but he fights it back unlike many who can turn it on and off over anything or nothing at all. If his seldom displayed emotions are an act, well he's the best actor I've seen in recent memory. He speaks from the heart, just as he did about his grandpa. The message he delivers is less cerebral and more from one heart to the hearts of others.

The heart, it's hard to discern which heart does what. I am not convinced that the heart that pumps blood and keeps us pink and above ground has any capability to emote. I've always thought it just a vital organ until four years ago when atrial fibrillation came my way after an emotional display of my own. So is the heart doing this thing or is the mind sending it the wrong signals? Is the heart we refer to located within the confines of our mind or is it generally located somewhere below the neck. I have heard others refer to certain individuals as heartless, an obvious mischaracterization of a person with a beating heart. The heart they refer to is obviously the one above the neck. It is the heart that is located somewhere inside the functioning mind. So this work will focus on this heart, the source of emotion and the place of stored feelings within the confines of the thinking, reasoning mind.

During my working life I had to control this heart of mine to refuse outward displays of emotions. While interviewing prospective employees often it was when in a serious moment, hilarious answers would come my way. L had to contain myself to a poker faced state else I might offend the prospect. Later it would resurface when alone or when I recounted the affairs of the day with my wife that the laughter would come through. One day an associate related to me a serious medical condition he was dealing with in hopes my registered nurse wife might provide some clinical direction. I respected, still do by the way, this guy a lot and thought she might help so I was willing to do what I could to help. It took a few minutes for him to get the courage to tell me what he thought he had. The word he used for the affliction was nothing short of absolutely hilarious. Though it took superior self control, and my heart was demanding an emotional outburst of epic proportions, my mind dictated otherwise and I was successful at containing myself until I got home later that evening. I won't relate the rest of the story as it is just too funny to recount on paper. I still think of that day often and laugh out loud. Even now as I write about it I'm laughing. Truly, you would've had to have been there!

My purpose here is really to distinguish the heart from the mind. I believe the heart we refer to most often is that repository of memories that are both good and bad. The heart is the part of us that exercises feelings. The mind refers to their images and our response to them often. The heart is also that part of us that displays facially our pleasure or displeasure. And our voice is the place this pleasure or displeasure is spoken of, laughed at or with and generally conveys our feelings. That's it!

The heart is the part of us that has feelings, not to be confused with the ability to feel objects or feel hot and cold. It's our heart that suffers when our feelings are hurt. It's our heart that experiences elation and pleasure when our feelings are pleasantly touched. Our heart experiences feelings. Those feelings often control our actions. But it often takes the mind to control these emotions when their display would be hurtful, inappropriate or just the wrong place and the wrong time. My mind has failed my heart on numerous occasions.

I am not too sure that the heart has an accomplished reasoning center. I believe it relies on our ability to read, hear, see, touch and reason to properly develop the heart's response to any and all situations. Those abilities are clearly within the mind's abilities to search out, receive and process to develop a proper response by the heart. My first attraction to my wife was literally in black and white. She was the fairest of the fair in our home county here in Tennessee. Her image from the pageant on the front page of the paper just screamed that she would be mine. It was strictly a base response of the heart. The mind had little involvement in the decision to seek her out. She was obviously very pretty, still is. She was all those things my heart told me I deserved. In a word, she was and is very beautiful. That motivation, provided by the heart, made it difficult for her to get to know me well enough for her to say yes to a marriage proposal. And for that very reason alone it made our dating difficult as I wanted to move along much faster than did she. But finally her mind delivered the verdict to her heart and my mind reconciled to my heart that it was finally the right time. It was difficult. Anyone that knows my wife will agree with the contention that she is difficult to influence if her heart and mind are not both on the same page. It took years for me to get that through my mind to my heart, literally decades.

The way our heart and mind interacts is not the same for all of us. I will often act out of a condition of the heart without much influence from my mind, a lifelong problem of mine. My wife on the other hand seldom acts out of emotion without first consulting her mind. Once I figured that out I wondered whether that was learned behavior or in the genes. I have reached no conclusion on that question though I would tend to believe that both play a role in forming our behavior, indeed the functioning of the heart and mind together. From personal experience I must conclude that I sometimes, maybe more often than not, act with too much of one and not enough of the other. The death of my son is a case in point.

Upon learning the news of his death I was immediately unable to cry or even display sadness. It took hours and hours to reach the conclusion that my son was dead, that he will never return to our home and that he has vacated the earth permanently. It seemed that the heart was just absent from the tragic event. But my mind was moving quite lethargically as well. Maybe it was just the shock of it all that disabled the normal response of sudden grief. Initially my mind had moved from the loss of my son to those things our family would soon face. Maybe it was a defense mechanism. Who knows! I was just that very day pronounced in remission from Wegener's Granulomatosis, my often spoken of deadly and incurable form of vasculitis, and was finding it difficult to handle the effects of high doses of corticosteroids, joint and muscle pain and months of sleep deprivation. Then the joy from learning I might not die in a few months elicited both an outward and inward show of relief. All this happened within just a few hours of my son's tragic death. It seemed my heart was questioning my mind with this question: What is wrong with you? Why could I not break into tears immediately upon the news that he had passed away? It just cannot be explained by "too much going on".

Looking back on that time, especially the night of the accident, I have concluded that the shock of the event coupled with the long term steroid use and the many problems that Alex's death brought to our family just overloaded my mind's ability to handle the situation with an immediate emotional response.

Something had to suffer. And it was my heart that took the backseat for a time, short as it was. It took my heart a good while to take over the proper emotional response to such a loss, indeed the greatest loss a father can experience. It really made up for lost time during the year that followed. I would find myself bursting into tears and even convulsive sobbing when alone. The sadness was overwhelming. Those that have experienced this kind of loss can easily understand just what I am conveying here. Those that have missed out on this experience, well, count your blessings.

The heart is very much like my stage 3b kidneys as one gastroenterologist related during an office visit. It is often not trustworthy. He indicated that my kidneys could fail me at most any time and that they were likely the most serious physical threat I face. The heart alone is not a sound means by which to reach important decisions, especially life and death decisions. Without a doubt, my heart alone is not trustworthy for the most important decision faced in life. The oversight and direction of the mind is critically necessary in the heart's exercise of the decision to follow Christ. I have heard it said many times that the mind must be eliminated in the decision to follow Jesus. Stressing further, that the heart alone was responsible for that considered decision. I could not disagree more!

Life's worst decisions stem from decisions made by the heart alone. The heart responds to appearance, desirability and physical stimuli in reaching what it believes to be a sound decision. It responds to pleasurable attention from others too. Often the undesirable results are undesirable lifelong changes that are sometimes life threatening and sometimes result in the death of self or others. The heart can make a decision alone but it takes the mind to provide the reasoning for the trust that is necessary for that decision to be sound. I believe with all my heart, soul and mind that might be the cause of Christianity's weak presence today. We have ill executed Christianity that resulted from decisions purely of the heart that failed to understand just what Christ did for us and why we needed Him. That understanding is vital. Just following the lead of someone else is not secure salvation. There must be consideration of what one is accepting and the genuine act of repentance. Neither of those is hard to do but both require the mind in executing them through the heart. I make this sound difficult but that is not my intention. I think it necessary to explore why we've degenerated to the point of making mindless decisions to reward the pulpit with what are often essentially just aisle walkers.

A man told me once that his third baptism was the result of his answer to the question from the pulpit "Are you going to hell?" He told me that he didn't want to go to hell so he "got baptized" for the third time. I think this happens a lot. Fear moves us to announce a decision that likely is very innocently disingenuous. Fear alone might one day save your life here on earth but fear alone cannot possibly save your soul from eternal separation from God. Forever is a long time to trust emotion alone with the decision to repent and follow Jesus. "I fear hell" is not the motivating factor. The heart responds to conviction as directed by the mind when the question is more than just avoiding physical pain in hell. It is with the mind that the two meet with a considered response to the question of following Christ that is life changing. Understanding one's actions, one's sin, and the need for redemption sparks the need for the heart to seek safety, to seek forgiveness.

"Are you sure that you are saved? Come up here and let's make sure that you're not going to hell" are words often heard from the pulpits of America. Will that do it? Will that save your soul? Of course not! That's just an easy way to harvest results on the part of some preachers and a lazy way to handle one's arrangements with Jesus, very likely a false sense of eternal security. Connecting with Jesus is not a decision not to go to hell nor is it a decision that heaven sounds good either. It is definitely not akin to selecting a place for an everlasting vacation. Both locations are consequences, physical destinations. They are not the question. The question the mind must consider is whether it is not just plausible, but that it is a certainty that Jesus was the Son of God. Realizing that one's own personal sin guilt, a debt beyond one's own means to pay, looms personally and eternally large is also necessary. Seeking out the sufficiency of sacrifice yields the only source for redemption: Jesus, the very Son of God, and the perfect Sacrifice. That's just not that hard. But it does require evaluation by the mind of the facts as the Bible relates them to us. And once that is a part of your life faith becomes the block on which a life pleasing to God can be cultivated. There is always more stuff for the mind to continually build into one's heart for God.

The cerebral gravity of just what Jesus did for us will require much study even after salvation. The looming question is why would Jesus come to earth to save me from my disobedience from God's commands? One can openly repent and believe that Jesus died to save you from your sins. That genuine act alone results in secure redemption through the work of Christ on the cross. And that is genuinely enough just for the consequence of heaven. Shaking the preacher's hand and reciting the sinner's prayer disingenuously will be just enough to result in the consequence of eternal separation from God. In a word, hell is your consequence. It is just too important and too easy to avoid consideration by the mind, the genuine meeting of one's own heart, soul and mind with that of Jesus. It is even a commandment to love God with all your heart, soul and mind.

"Master, which is the great commandment in the law? Jesus said unto him, Thou shalt love the Lord thy God with all thy heart, and with all thy soul, and with all thy mind. This is the first and great commandment." Matthew 22:36-38 KJV

A fruitful walk with Jesus will find the heart demanding answers to the questions of life. Why do bad things happen to good people? Did God suffer over His Son's crucifixion? Why did God not protect my son? Does God know everything? I mean really every single little thing? Is the Holy Spirit a real thing? How do I know when it is God speaking to me? How could God have created everything from nothingness? Why should I love Him?

Why does He love me is the larger question? God did love His creation of mankind so much that he sent His only Son to save it from itself. So why did it require the Son of God? That's the question that takes a little while to answer. But the unanswerable question in total is how do I know God better? And the answer is that you can know God better but you can never fully know all the attributes of God. And I think that is precisely why life enduring study of God's Word to us is vital in a growing understanding of God. The more I learn about God the more I realize there's just that much more to seek out.

It may just be me, but I am not motivated to study scripture by recommended daily Bible readings though I do believe they can be beneficial. I search for answers to these questions all the time in an effort to know God better. I am more a researcher for personal benefit. One day I will see Him face to Face and I hope I will know Him so well by then I will recognize Him instantly. I believe I will. The last two years I have engaged in a study of the New Testament studying by author. I started with Paul's inspired writing and moved through the other writers fairly smoothly. Of late I have been studying the Gospel of John, his three letters, and just this morning started on the Revelation of Jesus Christ to John. Continually studying the scriptures builds faith and a relationship with God that mindfully affirms the position of hope to a certainty that the Christian heart has. One can understand what Jesus did and believe and be saved without knowing all there is to know about God, but one must know Jesus to understand what He did and believe it, a joint endeavor by the mind and heart.

Our true and real relationship with God the Father, God's own Son and the Holy Spirit can be the thing, in fact the only thing, that brings everlasting peace, indeed everlasting life to the soul of man. I would assert that the mind is integral in providing the heart with the ammunition to genuinely call on the name of the Lord. And so why was the Son of God required to redeem us, to redeem me? Because it took one in kind, without blemish, to fully cover the sins of the world, even my own. And the Son of God was the only Way! Be mindful of the high price that was required for your sins.

For ye are bought with a price: therefore glorify God in your body, and in your spirit, which are God's. I Corinthians 6:20 KJV

Chapter 11

Old Shirts

A few days ago I walked into the closet to pick out a shirt to wear. My wife and I were going into town to have dinner. As I moved hangers left and right I selected a shirt that was probably five years old, maybe older. I can't remember exactly how old it was but it probably didn't match my shorts either. It was so impressive I can't even remember which one it was. However, I do remember not caring whether it was in style, whether it matched or whether or not anyone would notice that it was not exactly..... in vogue.

I have arthritis so I leave all my shirts buttoned up except for the collar band, which I only button if I plan on wearing a necktie, and the next button down the placket. In so doing, I don't have to fumble around with buttons with fingertips that have rotated about forty five degrees in the past few years. Pulling it over my head as I walked through the house I thought, who cares what this shirt looks like. It doesn't bother me that it might be out of style or even beyond the service life of the goods it was made from. It brought to mind a clearer understanding of a time long ago at my parents' home, probably forty years ago.

I would have been mid twenties at the time and full of myself more so back then than today. My dad was sitting outside. It was the time of glamour in the oilfield and of television shows that celebrated oilmen, cultivating widespread envy of the rich and powerful. In keeping with the time and my job I was wearing expensive black lizard skin cowboy boots, an oilfield belt buckle, a sea grass cowboy hat and no telling what else. But what I was wearing meant something if only to me and no one else. But it was the job and nothing more. It was important to dress the part to be taken seriously. I realized soon after that I was no more an oilman than I was president. Indeed, I was all hat and no cattle.

Dad was recently retired and a responsible man of some means yet not rich. My brother and sisters and I always thought our parents were rich. I guess the way in which they provided for us sent that message. Anyway, my parents didn't do without as far as I could tell but they were by no means rich. As I approached dad as he sat on the deck I noticed what he was wearing. I was in my $275 (a lot at the time) boots. He was wearing an obviously worn out pair of khaki trousers and a pair of gym shoes he bought at a discount store for four dollars, surely a blue light special. The shoes were the kind that would not provide traction on any surface, wet or dry, and would immediately draw pity from any observer. Dad wore a size six shoe so maybe that's all he could find though I seriously doubt it.

The khaki trousers were along the fashion lines of that of a carpenter. You know, the big wide belt loops and baggy legs, a loop for a claw hammer, with stains from years of gardening and mowing grandma's cemetery lot way down under the mountain. For those who have never lived on the Cumberland Plateau, under the mountain means off of the plateau. Those clothes were beyond the point of making useful grease rags. I remember the weather being hot that day, probably early summer and probably on a Saturday. So I thought it a bit hot to be sitting outside in a pair of long pants........ wearing his white ball shoes........and wearing that shirt.

That shirt! It was so absolutely tasteless and probably cost a couple of dollars and that would've been grossly overpriced. It was a washed out teal plaid with a pattern repeat of at least six or seven inches. At least it was short sleeved and was about the right weight for the time of year and the temperature and humidity Tennessee is known for. Most of the color had been washed down to earth tones and the shirt would've easily passed for worn out India madras though in reality it was a broadcloth blend of polyester and cotton. I'm sure of it. A few years later I would be an executive in the shirt business so I know my shirts, at least that kind of shirt.

Walking through the house, pulling my shirt over my head, I realized that it could easily have been a shirt my dad would have worn at about that point in his life where I find myself just now. There's nothing cheap about me but my clothes. As a matter of fact, the shorts I put on that morning were green cargo shorts and the waistband button pulled off just as I buttoned it. Yes, another entry for the grease rag basket in the shop. But wait, no, I would repair them! They are my favorite pair of work shorts and you can wear them anytime, anywhere so I thought. So, as I write, they are on the chair in the bedroom awaiting needle, thread, and my unpracticed hands sewing the button back on. It's not my first rodeo salvaging an otherwise worthless garment.

So why am I taking this position? Why save the worn out shorts? Why wear the hideous shirt selected from a closet full of very nice sport shirts? Why am I now dressing in the fashion palette, though very different, of my dad forty years later without a thought of my disdain for the way he was clothed that day. So I thought on that for a little while. As I worked in the garden and checked on my honey bees that day, in the out of style, worn out, off the rack shirt, in my lace up army boots, I realized why. It just wasn't important anymore. What I wore and who saw me just did not matter anymore. In the grand scheme of things it really never did.

There was a day I wore expensive cowboy boots every day, a big belt buckle, and all that sometimes with a coat and tie. There was another time in my life I wore custom made shirts, made in a factory I managed, expensive Italian silk ties compliments of a name brand necktie designer in New York, and an eel skin belt. Still another time I was in steel toed work boots wearing the cheapest blue jeans money could buy and a shirt that would be ok with being caught up in a metalworking machine or welding burnt and ruined. And finally, a day I dress as I wanted but never exactly tacky, just whatever was comfortable and cleanly pressed. There was an image to project, an image unlike any others in the industries I had worked in, all of them. And now, well, really the last ten years or so, image has meant nothing. You know, it never did mean a thing. It just wasn't important then and it is truly meaningless now.

Just this morning I was in a white beekeeping jacket, white painters pants and an olive drab tee shirt from the souvenir shop at the Alamo in San Antonio. My zip-up canvas army boots were on with my pant legs held tight around my boot tops by a hook and loop strap hopefully to prevent a wayward bee from ruining my morning while I cut the grass at the beehives. A fashion statement? Of course not! It's just that these are the only garments I have that really have a specific use and mean something for a particular appearance or purpose. New or old, in style or absolutely the tackiest, it just doesn't matter anymore. I have reached that stage my dad was in forty years ago. And finally, I believe I understand.

Maybe it was different for him than for me. But as I have said many times, most assuredly, every day is a good day to go to heaven and today is no exception. I am always dressed for that. And what does one wear to go to heaven? You put on the armor of God. It never goes out of style, is always available and is eternally invincible. The armor of God is not available in any store that I am aware of. It's more a set of armor found in the prescription for living and dying found in, and only in, the Word of God. My armor has a few holes in it but His is impenetrable. I am working on my armor so that it more resembles His in function and appearance. This armor, how does one explain it? Well, I can only give my own explanation but here it is as far as I can see to tell you.

It doesn't necessarily start with creation but that's a good place to start. The first mention of anything in the Bible is the creation fact. Wait now, I failed to call it the creation story. If only a story then it might not stand up to reason or question. Creation by God in my mind has been accepted as fact, not a story left to a personal belief or interpretation. I've studied the Bible enough and personally observed creation sufficiently to arrive at a solid conviction that it is sound for factual belief. If any of the Bible is unreliable then it's all brought into question. I differ with those who would suggest that inconsistencies and outright fabrications are found throughout the Bible. And many will scoff at my total belief in everything I find therein. That's fine with me. I won't have to explain myself to them.

The display of power in creation is of such enormity as to be without challenge for greatness. In the very beginning the earth was without form and there was only darkness. God spoke light into being and separated the light from darkness all on the first day. That's quite an act of creation and a lot of work all in a day. Without light there can be no life, no photosynthesis, no food chain, no warmth....no energy. God separated the liquid water from the gaseous water, sustaining it in the atmosphere implicit with His work on the second day. And the third day, He brought forth the land by gathering the water. Vegetation, plant life, came into being on the same day. The bodies in outer space were created, also the sun and moon, on the fourth day. Sea life and fowl were the continuing creative work for the next day, the fifth day. And on day six God created the land animals, mankind and everything else that was created. Six days, all that was, is, and ever shall be, God created. He set in motion all that is creation. That's power! That's all the power that was. That's all the power that is. Power, all of it, was provided for at the time of creation, all emanating from God.

Is creation, the act of creation, the fact of creation, part of the armor? You bet it is! Without a belief to a certainty that God did what is recorded in Genesis one cannot rely on the armor of God being sufficient to keep that which is us, our very souls, in an environment of everlasting life as He so promised to do over and over. If He is not the Master of creation then there would be credible doubt in His competence to provide a piece of armor. If He is not what He says He is, if He didn't do what the Bible says He did, then the reliability of that armor is indeed suspect. We should not cower under the threat of, or actual act of ridicule that comes from non believers. As cited before, what is seen in creation should leave even the strongest scoffer in awe and with a conviction that creation is indeed an act of Divinity, the display of, and act of an all powerful God.

He gave us choice, a will of our own. Created in His image, I expect free will was part of that image. I believe He gave us the ability to exercise our free will with competence. The willingness to so exercise it seems to be quite weak. Instinctively, we know what the will should be but we seem to overemphasize the free part. Willful disregard for what God gave us as standards for living has produced disastrous use of free will.

God expected little and gave much to Adam and Eve. He gave them life. He gave them a wonderful place to live and dominion over everything that lived and breathed. I envy their view of the yet unspoiled earth. The simplicity of the life they lived and the natural beauty of the earth yet without a curse must have been absolutely breathtaking. We want it our way regardless of the way God willed it. It was a losing hand then and it is a losing hand today though we still practice our hand at being God with almost a willful disregard for the consequences. We all know the factual result. The earth was cursed and the relationship that Adam and Eve had with God would never be the same again. Toil and pain entered their lives for the first time. But it would not be the last.

All through Biblical, factual history, man rebelled. Man was disobedient. It seems as if, and is likely true, that we have rebelled much, much more often than obeyed. Arrogantly, man has always seemed to task God to do what He must to be what He is: All Powerful, Sovereign, absolutely Just, and the Author of Truth without compromise. You know that compromise is never optimal. Compromise is agreement of less than optimal, less than right policy for the purposes of expedience. God gave us sound guidance. Thou shalt love the Lord thy God. Love thy neighbor. Judge not. Do not kill, steal or witness falsely against a neighbor. Very obviously, this is not an exhaustive list of commandments. The list of things God gave us as commands by which to live is rather brief but totally comprehensive. We pick and choose. We as a species always have. And it has never ended well.

The world became so rebellious, so wicked, that God destroyed it in a flood. All that survived of the human race was Noah, his wife, their three sons and their wives. It took decades for Noah to build the ark. And more recent in history, just a few hundred years later in fact, God would destroy Sodom and Gomorrah. The Bible is a bloody book recounting the history of our free will choices and the consequences thereof. The Hebrew people found themselves in and out of captivity more than once. In a word, sin. All of the world's problems, all of the world's suffering can be traced back to one thing. Sin.

"The earth also was corrupt before God, and the earth was filled with violence. And God looked upon the earth, and, behold, it was corrupt; for all flesh had corrupted his way upon the earth. And God said unto Noah, The end of all flesh is come before me; for the earth is filled with violence through them; and, behold, I will destroy them with the earth." Genesis 6:11-13 KJV

We just can't seem to understand that God must deliver. To be what God claims to be He must be absolutely just and purely truthful. He can be neither if He fails to do what He said He would do even once. He must stick to His word. If the wages of sin is death, then death it is and death it must be. Otherwise, God would just be making a threat. God makes promises not threats. I am glad His Word is a promise otherwise the promise of salvation might just be a threat. But for that and many, many other reasons I can count on God to be as good as His Word. He didn't threaten everlasting life. He promised it. He always means what He says. He promised it if only I would place my trust in His Son. And I did so never wondering if He would follow through. That's what He does. I know that because I know He means what He says every time, all the time. If He said it you can count on it. It might just appear harsh to us but if He failed to deliver on anything He has said, well, you wouldn't know which part to rely on and which part you could not. But as it is, as He is, His promise of everlasting life is as solid as anything could possibly be and He proves it over and over by delivering without prejudice His promise to all who would so believe.

So what about this armor of God? Understanding God and wearing the armor comes with understanding His Word. We are the most privileged people in all of history. We have the Bible. Initially, the Word of God was passed mouth to ear. Later it was recorded as inspired writers provided more and more revealed Word of God. We've got it all! Salvation comes through a penitent trust in Jesus, but the armor of God comes from continuing study of God and His Son, their words, their actions and a sold out knowledge that it is entirely fact, not just a collection of stories that might or might not have any truth in them. Even the parables, clearly stories and identified as such in scripture, had a purpose in factually teaching the intent of God's Word. God's Word is not subject to our approval or agreement.

There is much to be gained by studying the divine Word of God. Captivity and deliverance and the reasons for both are on colorful display on the pages of both the Old and New Testaments. The covenantal relationship between God and His people is stressed throughout scripture. The armor of God is a read-study-and-prayed-on spiritual coating that builds our defenses against temptation and the acts of sin that we face every day of our lives. It's a truth and consequences spiritual narrative that goes on within each of us. Faced with the temptation to steal or cheat, for example, we are reminded in scripture of the consequences of such actions. Moreover, as far as consequences go, the big sin and the little sin carry the same penalty - death, separation from God forever. Disobedience brings chastisement. It might be delayed for a long time but it will come. It will be permanent. It will be forever. It will be unbearable yet must be endured forever. As one builds up that armor, commits to that truth, the fact of scripture, it's absolute reliability will become more and more clear and one will be less inclined to yield to temptation.

The one piece of God's armor that one must put on, must claim, must possess, is the relationship of Christ through repentance and total, unfailing belief that He, Jesus, died in payment of our sins, yours and mine. Without that piece of armor one is not in danger of separation from God but is indeed already separated from God, will forever be separated from God and will reside in everlasting torment after death. No other article of armor will provide the avenue to everlasting life in the very presence of God forever. One can possess all the understanding in scripture that is humanly possible but failing to have Christ as the helmet, one might resist sin yet miss the eternal reward found through Christ and only through Christ.

Understanding the facts, mindfully considering what is contained in scripture arms one with the truth, the truth according to God. The only truth, the truth that matters, is the truth according to God, the truth that enables one to stand up to the evil forces of this world. The truth that builds and strengthens faith becomes the breast plate of one's armor. And Christ, through our belief on and in the Son of God, the helmet of salvation, completes our growing, real, personal relationship with God.

Dad's shirt just didn't matter to him anymore nor did my selection of what to wear forty years later. One of my dad's last statements before he died was, "How can God ever forgive me for the things I've done?" I knew dad to be a man of strong faith. I knew he was imperfect and yielded to sin just as have I. But I knew he had a strong set of armor. I also knew that he had the helmet of Christ in his spiritual wardrobe. I do too. I knew dad knew the answer. He knew his sins were covered by the blood. The things of this world take on much less luster as one becomes focused, mindfully settled, on everlasting life. And he was right at the door.

Moving from life on this earth to heaven is a longing of mine. To be totally honest, I do fear the event of dying a little bit. But I've studied the facts presented to me in the Bible and I can't wait to get to heaven. As long as I am working on my armor here, helmeted with the blood of Christ, I am certain that my armor will see me through. This armor, the armor of God, is only available from God. I pray that He strengthens my armor more every day. I pray that I seek His armor and that I never am satisfied with my place in the word. I need it. I need it every day! Put on the armor!

"Finally, my brethren, be strong in the Lord, and in the power of his might. Put on the whole armour of God, that ye may be able to stand against the wiles of the devil. For we wrestle not against flesh and blood, but against principalities, against powers, against the rulers of the darkness of this world, against spiritual wickedness in high *places*. Wherefore take unto you the whole armour of God, that ye may be able to withstand in the evil day, and having done all, to stand.

Stand therefore, having your loins girt about with truth, and having on the breastplate of righteousness;   And your feet shod with the preparation of the gospel of peace;   Above all, taking the shield of faith, wherewith ye shall be able to quench all the fiery darts of the wicked.   And take the helmet of salvation, and the sword of the Spirit, which is the word of God: Praying always with all prayer and supplication in the Spirit, and watching thereunto with all perseverance and supplication for all saints." Ephesians 6:10-18 KJV

Chapter 12

The Woman and the Broken Flask

"And being in Bethany in the house of Simon the leper, as he sat at meat, there came a woman having an alabaster box of ointment of spikenard very precious; and she brake the box, and poured it on his head. And there were some that had indignation within themselves, and said, Why was this waste of the ointment made? For it might have been sold for more than three hundred pence, and have been given to the poor. And they murmured against her. And Jesus said, Let her alone; why trouble ye her? she hath wrought a good work on me. For ye have the poor with you always, and whensoever ye will ye may do them good: but me ye have not always."
Mark 14: 3-7 KJV

Don't we do this now? I mean question those things others do for Christ? Of course we do. I do. You do. We all do. But laying aside the questioning of the actions of others, what have I done to honor Jesus as had the woman in this text? This is where the spiritual rubber hits the road. Doing things for Jesus can be a difficult road. In this passage the woman lavishly anoints Jesus in the present view of others and is criticized even in front of Jesus. Jesus chastises them and honors the woman's actions.

It's all but impossible for you and me to have the very same experience. Jesus is not here in the body for a physical show of love directly to Him. That just is not a possibility. But would we if we could? And if we did do it would it be for the right reasons? Would our motivations be sound? I really don't know and will never know the intentions of others. Especially in this day of spinning everything into something it's not just for appearances or to voice a political stance. Jesus, the ultimate and infallible judge, knows this woman's intentions and finds them sound. He knows her heart, something we cannot possibly know.

Church, well organized religion, has become big business in the last years. Television preachers living in mansions, flying around the world in private jets and hoarding cash by reaping the well intentioned anointing of Jesus head. If you've done it to the least of these you've done it unto me really takes on new meaning here. It's indeed difficult to show love and affection and dedication and lend comfort to Jesus through the symbol of the church in keeping with the spirit on display by this woman. That she acted publicly truly presents a problem in today's world. I choose not to engage publicly in displays of giving to the church, or engaging in benevolent acts in the view of others toward the poor and less fortunate.

"Take heed that ye do not your alms before men, to be seen of them: otherwise ye have no reward of your Father which is in heaven. Therefore when thou doest thine alms, do not sound a trumpet before thee, as the hypocrites do in the synagogues and in the streets, that they may have glory of men. Verily I say unto you, They have their reward. But when thou doest alms, let not thy left hand know what thy right hand doeth: That thine alms may be in secret: and thy Father which seeth in secret himself." Matthew 6:1-4 KJV

It's almost impossible for the left hand not to know what the right hand is doing. Tax deductions require documentation and that documentation must be affirmed by a third party, particularly the receiving party. For that reason and others I have chosen to take the standard deduction for federal income taxes rather than itemize deductions so as to shield my charitable acts and tithes from government scrutiny, even under audit. So should we leave a bag of cash in the sanctuary under cover of darkness only to be recorded as an anonymous gift to the church, totally outside the knowledge of one hand or another? See, that's how things are so easily conflicted.

The act of this woman had little or nothing to do with stewardship. It did not appear to be of any further use than just for the immediate and temporary gratification of Jesus himself. I believe that is a very different thing than stewardship. She outwardly and physically worshipped Jesus, and at some cost to her. Some might argue that we can't do that today. I probably would have attempted that argument myself until just now. Could I, would I if I could? Can I, will I if I can? I would like to think I could and I would.

Does reaping a little enjoyment while engaging in benevolent acts negate the service to God? There are so many fine lines in this subject and so few guidelines to be guided by. In the case of the woman and the flask of ointment I would suggest that her pleasure was entirely found in the pleasure Jesus experienced while she poured it on his head. Additionally, those present likely caused her embarrassment when they suggested that what she was doing had a higher and better use. I think they were wrong. So if they were wrong, how does that affect service acts today?

Churches today have gyms, locker rooms, commercial kitchens, playgrounds complete with equipment, buses and most have money, some of them quite a bit of dough. I'm not suggesting these things are bad but I believe they can become the subject of church sanctioned idolatry. They can become highly protected items purely for the enjoyment and pleasure of those that use it, sometimes even a select minority of a congregation. Though I am a couple thousand years beyond the period I am writing about I long to see today's churches return to the first century model. It will not. I expect, and scripture suggests, that the church will actually become apostate. It would appear to be headed in that direction right before our eyes.

Some churches send the wrong message. My middle sister has asked me several times why churches refuse their facilities to the homeless during inclement weather. That's a very hard question to answer and I'm sure not all churches do that. I have never been satisfied with my answer because these people would certainly be in the "least of these" class of those Jesus is concerned with. Are we denying them even a cup of cool water and are we doing it to Jesus himself in the process? My answer to her is that the homeless sometimes cause damage in the facilities, steal things and abuse the privilege that those churches that provide the privilege provide. There is not a correct answer to have a gymnasium complete with showers, a commercial kitchen complete with cupboards and freezers full of food that are denied to the needy and freezing. And as I turn the mirror on myself, I find I am just as guilty as anyone. I am ashamed of that too. I would suggest that the mind sometimes overrules the better judgment of the heart.

Missions away from the home campus of a church deserve a little scrutiny too. It is no longer necessary to fly to an island in the Caribbean to view the poor. They exist right here, just a few miles from my home. Some of these foreign missions are quite good. I believe Samaritan's Purse does an outstanding job on the missions they do. That organization finds itself in areas where spreading the gospel might be lacking or even totally absent such as war zones, natural disasters and extreme poverty. Their missions are anything but beach or amusement park glazed trips. They certainly appear to be good stewards of the money entrusted to their use. If some are offended, I am sorry. But if my building needs a roof, please don't send me a bunch of high school students. Send me those with the skills necessary to meet the need or the money to hire some local skilled labor with steel toed boots, saws and hammers.

It is not to say that student mission trips are bad. Leadership often fashions these trips near vacation spots in an effort to attract the "unchurched". As a friend once said to me, "If it takes a free hotdog, chips and a soft drink to get them in church, when you withdraw the freebee they will likely disappear". But it sure makes our heart feel good now doesn't it. What would it say for someone passing by to see a church youth group gathering trash off the side of the road or cleaning up an illegal dump, removing graffiti from natural beauty or raking the yard of an elderly couple? Undoubtedly it would speak volumes. No beach day or no day at Disney would likely dwindle down the participants in missions such as those.

Playing team sports in church attracts hundreds of people to the church gymnasium. Really, who is not going to see their son or daughter or grandkid play basketball? Certainly, I will. But I go to church anyway. I suspect most of the participants are already church members. Hundreds of thousands of dollars, even millions, are spent on these facilities. Then scoreboards, uniforms, multiple basketballs, snack bars, showers, bleachers and better floors than the local high school plays on are added to the cost. Walking tracks are very often added to soften the financial blow to the lifers in church. And I honestly don't see a thing wrong with the concept but I question the stewardship sometimes.

When I was a kid, we played hide and go seek outside the church. Kick the can was also a hot activity, requiring a spent soft drink can and a few kids. We played touch football and basketball on the church grounds. And a layperson would give a real devotional before the activity. That's not to say that these activities didn't attract people to the church. They did. But it was the gospel preached that kept them there. Of course the gospel is still preached in churches today, but the presentation to the mind of the believer has dwindled down from presenting the gospel to marketing Jesus. Jesus is not for sale. We are! He bought us with His own faultless blood. I do believe our minds and wealth have led us astray from the highest and best means by which to deliver the gospel, all with the blessing of our hearts. We are very effective at producing warm and fuzzy feelings.

The government could not have been more clever in circumventing the benevolent acts of the church. If you don't have it, there's likely a government program for you to get it whether you need it or not. The church now only slightly views its job of ministering to the poor and needy, the homeless, the abusers of drugs, and the sick and mentally ill. The government has a program for it, all of it. I would assert that the government is rarely the best vehicle by which to minister to those in need. But it has the appearance of relieving the church from those things Christ would have us do. Now, with the government doing the work, the church has reaped a government dividend. But the government leaves the critical element out in its delivery of services: the gospel. Instead of the army of God providing assistance, living out the commandments, and presenting the gospel, well, we are off the hook. We can let the government do the job while making people dependent on the government instead of looking to Christ.

We are supposed to be in and have fellowship in the church. And we can sure do it. The line between corporate Christian fellowship and nothing more than social interaction has certainly blurred. I have developed a disciplined approach to the study of scripture and devotion. There was a time I really enjoyed church gatherings, Sunday school classes and other church sanctioned functions. Disease and a permanently immunocompromised physical condition required that I abandon most things of a social or fellowship order at church. When my disease was most active a common cold was life threatening. So I developed a class of my own. I am the only member of the class and the Bible is my teacher. I expect I should be more critical of myself in this regard. Necessity, indeed, was the mother of invention and my spiritual needs were mostly met alone with the sixty six volumes we call the Bible.

The main event for me is the preaching. I have been blessed in life to sit before several very good preachers, a couple even considered great by my heavily discerning ears, eyes and mind. There was a time I felt guilt when I missed preaching on Sunday. I still do once again. Guilt has been replaced by a drive to hear preaching. The church we attend still has both morning and evening services on Sunday and a very sound broadcast system together with the skilled lay people to make it easy, almost without excuse, to never miss preaching. During cold weather and times of spreading flu, covid and other viral threats I choose to take advantage of the broadcasted preaching. I will say though that there is no substitute to hearing the Word of God preached face to face. I am presently fortunate to sit before the most capable, always prepared, never redundant, gifted speaker of a preacher. That takes all the guilt away when one avails himself to the preached word whenever it is available.

But it's also not just the preacher I hear with the formal title of senior pastor that brings the word. After I wrote my first book, "Will I Have Wings" I asked a longtime friend to read my manuscript for content. I greatly respected his knowledge of scripture having heard him preach several times. He is one of the very best speakers I've ever heard. Through the years he and I have discussed many matters of theology and doctrine and our views are very similar. I have several, I guess you would say scriptural mentors that I listen to and prove with scripture. Though my faith in Christ's ability to cover my sins, a heartfelt conviction indeed, is unshakeable, my interest in just what Christ did for me only gets stronger. I continue to study and learn new things drawn from scripture, my understanding continues to grow and my feeling of knowing God gets more solid all the time.

In the final analysis, we are called to spread the gospel. Jesus himself called us to do that very thing. Invariably, when in a conversation with someone, presenting the gospel, questions come up about other things. Are you sure creation only took six days? Did the sea really part or did they wade across from one side to the other in a shallow area? Was the flood worldwide? Were Sodom and Gomorrah real places or just a story? Was Elijah taken to heaven in a whirlwind? Was Mary the mother of Jesus really a virgin? Is it true that Jesus never sinned? Was Paul a disciple or an apostle and what is the difference? Why was King David a man after God's own heart? There are so many questions that a lifetime in search of all the answers wouldn't cover all the bases. But a lifetime of study is well worth the effort to know God better and better. All the questions are answered in the Bible, maybe not to our agreement, but within the will of God.

Now back to the church. Don't take my criticism of the church things as an indictment of the church. It's neither meant to be nor would it be true to allege such a blanket allegation. It is simply meant to be no more than constructive. The purpose of the church is to love and praise God and spread the gospel to the ends of the earth. I believe my church covers those bases like a fog. Sure, like anything else, improvements can always be made and should be made. We should be vigilant in our efforts to make sure those things the church engages in fit within praise, worship and spreading the good news. The mind must be engaged together with the heart, as the soul prayerfully seeks divine direction, to be optimal in the function of the church. It's not all the heart nor is it entirely the mind. It's recognizing us in service to God, by the leadership of the Holy Spirit in all matters in a heartfelt, mindful endeavor of the soul together as a united body in Christ. Simply put, preaching Jesus and Him slain is the business of the church.

"Unto me, who am less than the least of all saints, is this grace given, that I should preach among the Gentiles the unsearchable riches of Christ; And to make all men see what is the fellowship of the mystery, which from the beginning of the world hath been hid in God, who created all things by Jesus Christ: To the intent that now unto the principalities and powers in heavenly places might be known by the church the manifold wisdom of God, According to the eternal purpose which he purposed in Christ Jesus our Lord: In whom we have boldness and access with confidence by the faith of him."
Ephesians 3:8-11 KJV

Unlike the woman anointing Jesus' head, we don't have Jesus with us in the flesh so to speak. We anoint his wishes by spreading the gospel, the good news. We do it unto Him when we do it to the least. A cup of cool water to the burning soul is our act of anointing Jesus. And one day I fully expect we, the believers in Christ, will have the same opportunity to anoint the head of our Savior face to Face. Until that day we must seek to understand all we can to make spreading the gospel all the more effective, building up the strength of our love for Him within the heart. It's soul building, soul building for the building of Christ's church of believers. It's both a heart and mind thing engaging the soul.

"When the Son of man shall come in his glory, and all the holy angels with him, then shall he sit upon the throne of his glory: And before him shall be gathered all nations: and he shall separate them one from another, as a shepherd divideth his sheep from the goats: And he shall set the sheep on his right hand, but the goats on the left. Then shall the King say unto them on his right hand, Come, ye blessed of my Father, inherit the kingdom prepared for you from the foundation of the world: For I was an hungered, and ye gave me meat: I was thirsty, and ye gave me drink: I was a stranger, and ye took me

in: Naked, and ye clothed me: I was sick, and ye visited me: I was in prison, and ye came unto me. Then shall the righteous answer him, saying, Lord, when saw we thee an hungered, and fed thee? or thirsty, and gave thee drink? When saw we thee a stranger, and took thee in? or naked, and clothed thee? Or when saw we thee sick, or in prison, and came unto thee? And the King shall answer and say unto them, Verily I say unto you, Inasmuch as ye have done it unto one of the least of these my brethren, ye have done it unto me." Matthew 25:31-40 KJV

"Go ye therefore, and teach all the nations, baptizing them in the name of the Father, and of the Son, and of the Holy Ghost: Teaching them to observe all things whatsoever I have commanded you: and, lo, I am with you alway, even unto the end of the world. Amen." Matthew 28:19-20 KJV

Chapter 13

Checking the Boxes

Therefore also now, saith the Lord, turn ye even to me with all your heart, and with fasting, and with weeping, and with mourning - Joel 2:12 KJV

Do you just ever read the same passages over and over through the years without pondering on the action suggested by any particular passage? Without realizing it I have done just that thing. I have done it a lot and for a long time and I suspect I'm not alone in the failing. I suppose it became a habit by reading the Bible for the purpose of checking off a spiritual condition box when in fact, it became reading for that purpose alone. Reading the Bible can become just a mindless activity like having the television on while sleeping. Guilty, yes, I'm guilty. That's just one of a whole multitude of reasons it's so important to be under the teaching and preaching of a competent and called pastor, one that challenges the listener with each point of the sermon. We need much less box checking and a lot more mindful study of scripture, study resulting in action.

While I was writing my first book "Will I Have Wings?" the challenge came from the pulpit again. I kept hearing this thing about fasting which I had relegated to the back burner as a largely archaic practice better left in the first century and earlier. On and off for more than a year I kept hearing this call to fast. It finally broke through the ice of my mind and I buckled down and studied it to gain an understanding of why and how to properly fast. As I studied I felt that it would be really easy to put this in the box checking category too. It would seem that today's Christian has too much box checking and too little actual interaction with and focused action for a loving God. I really don't want to find myself with page after page of checked boxes as proof of my love for God when I find myself giving account. We're not putting a puzzle together here. A devotional can be just as mindless as box checking itself. A focused conscious connection to God in all things checks all the boxes without a prescription so to do.

So in my first book I had a much abbreviated chapter about fasting that really just displayed my questions about the practice. Since writing that book I have actually engaged in the practice and think, though it was my first exposure to fasting in practice, that I achieved that focused engagement with God during the fast. A refined version of my first fast continues from time to time even as I key these words. It has changed my life. And it's not just my everyday life, it changed my physical life. Fasting has effected a growing relationship with God in my life. I thought that not possible until I experienced it firsthand. Thinking it through, I believe, that in preparing for fasting one would be wise to study the fasts of Christ. Forty days is a serious fast, one my doctors would argue would be foolish and life threatening for me. The more I engage in the practice the less I agree with the doctors.

That argument, seemingly a competitive argument, I feel loses the point entirely for any fast I might engage in. Fasting as a competition with Christ's fasting practices, though I suppose admirable, would lose focus entirely on why I would be fasting. I can't compete with Christ on anything. So I did what I thought I was called to do as I engaged in prayerful consideration, listening to the pastor and studying passages of scripture for how to fast with a view toward a focused connection with God. And that is not a box checking thing. It is hearing the Word of God preached, studying scripture and responding to the listening end of prayer. It's not a devotional as we box check now. It's a devotion sensed by and maybe only by God.

With my resident diseases, fasting must be carefully planned. Rather than martyr myself in the process, which would go largely unnoticed or termed foolish, the design of the fast had to be medically considered. Though I had never engaged in fasting as such, I had engaged in fasting as a clinical practice. Quoting now from "Will I Have Wings": "Both times I was in the induction phase for remission of Wegener's; I was forced to give up a lot. No processed sugar, no white bread, very little coffee, no red meat, no soft drinks. My meals for months were pretty much a hand prepared meal with water or diet cranberry juice to drink. If I never eat another blueberry, that works for me. I had to remove myself from close public contact, even from my daughter and grandson. Had it not been for the need of a twenty-four hour nurse at times, I would have had to stay away from my wife. But all that was not spiritually motivated. It was not an act of spiritual discipline. It was required of me to live without furthering the damage to my organs, becoming diabetic, or winding up a fatality due to an infection. During both episodes I lost weight despite long term use of high dosage steroids. And I became more aware of the spiritual oneness I could have with God though it wasn't a voluntary fast. It was prescribed and enforced by my wife. So I know firsthand that it had great benefit physically for me, but I did not enjoy it at all.

Fasting can be a diet of just fruits, nuts, vegetables and water. So over lunch not too long ago, my wife explained some of the peculiarities with this type of diet for me. One that immediately came to mind without her mentioning it was no bacon, no eggs, and I could forget about pancakes and French toast. Just think for a minute about the discipline this would take. Cutting down to just those food groups would likely be a failing for me. As she pointed out, it doesn't work if you eat six packs of nuts and six or eight pieces of fruit. And no, honey is not a fruit, a nut or a vegetable and it surely isn't water. I eat honey every morning.

And so fruits are full of potassium which is a heart no-no for me. So one must take fasting smartly and with due consideration.

But comparing me now with those periods in my life, fasting even involuntarily provided great physical benefit. So now I'm faced with the conviction that I should practice fasting on occasion, healthy or otherwise. I believe it will be beneficial to my prayer and study life. I might even listen better. I know it will be of benefit if I practice it with the degree of faith and discipline required. I consulted with my lead doctor to see what part of the practice I can do without removing myself as a living witness entirely.

It's about that you know, being a witness. What good are we if we are only good to and for ourselves? If we are of no benefit to mankind, if we are poor stewards, if there is no sacrifice in our lives, we just might as well go on to that somewhere we are going to forever. I've got a lot of growing in faith and nearing myself to God to do and a lot less time to do it than before. And I shall prayerfully try to the extent I'm able." Fasting is the graduate school of Christian discipline.

So what distinguishes fasting from just a garden variety diet? And do we classify one as the other which amounts in my opinion to spiritual counterfeiting? If it's essentially for losing weight without the spiritual discipline and prayerful forethought, meditation and reflection on what Christ did for us then it's just a diet and only a diet. There seems to be mindful continuity of faithful dedication that even presents an eagerness to fast that separates fasting from dieting. I cannot imagine finding myself eager to avoid doughnuts, cookies, cake and ice cream or sweet tea and fried foods. But I believe that eagerness is implicit in a true and faithful fast as if that eagerness manifests itself in a desire to please the Lord with a private show of faith and discipline.

So my pastor solicited the participation of all the members of our church, and any others in hearing, in an annual fast for just a few weeks. I felt I just had to fast. I do feel compelled to act on the word conveyed by the pastor. I avoided being foolish and trying a complete fast, an act that likely would have ended in death in just a few days considering my health issues. Where is the glory for God in that! So having discussed the matter with one of my doctors I decided to start a few days before the other members of the church planned to begin their fast. I had a battery of blood tests that would happen in late January and wanted to be finished with fasting a few days before.

I didn't tell anyone except my wife and the pastor what the particulars of my fast were. I only told the pastor because he asked and I was looking for any indication of disapproval in his words or tone. As it turned out, his fast was very similar to mine. My fast was between God and me, not between me and the other members of the church and not for comparison purposes either. And....I'm not going to tell you what my fasting terms were either. They will remain between God and me, my wife and the preacher. Suffice it to say that I selected things that I dearly love after a prayer for direction. I chose things that would be hard for me to give up. My selections would require a discipline I had not been used to in my diet. The things I chose to fast were hard choices for me, things that required a good bit of sacrifice on my part.

But what would be the elements of my fast? I'm not yet onboard with fasting things that aren't food or permanently parts of daily life. Somehow it loses something as I deliberate what to fast myself. I won't be critical of those that do but I wonder about it. There was no internet when Jesus walked the earth, no social media, no television. But I suppose we find ourselves in a day and time where they have become almost necessities in our daily lives, inseparable from daily routines without some level of sacrifice. Contrary to the evidence, I can do without social media. Even the news has become almost self abuse to watch what masquerades as news today. I'm of the opinion that an element of a fast must require the forbearing of something that is routine and normal and not something we should abstain from otherwise. For example, to abstain from binge drinking or gluttony or lethargy would not be elements of a fast at all. Indeed, they would be desirable life changes certainly requiring a keen discipline to accomplish, but not elements of a fast. I believe one of the things that separate a fasting element from a change for health reasons is the intent to resume consumption at a point in time.

Should it be at least a little bit of sacrifice on my part? I'm almost ashamed to use the term sacrifice when I immediately compare the sacrifice Christ made for me. He gave life itself and He did it for me as if for no one else. Wouldn't it have been more obvious had he displayed his power more forcefully by violent means than by love? Maybe so, but it would have been out of character for a loving God for the purpose intended.

So as I carefully considered the elements of my fast I couldn't help but compare the small sacrifice each, and even the entire list of elements was in comparison to the blood. Even Jesus' life itself, was sacrificed for me. Maybe that process involves a bit of rending of one's heart. It seems so little, fasting, in comparison with the price paid for me. I was sad that my fast seemed so spiritually anemic stacked up to the price Jesus paid for me. But finally I understood that the act, and a private act it was, of disciplined behavior in denying oneself those things held highly in our daily lives displayed an act of dedication and discipline in my faith.

So I started my fast. One month in and things were going quite well. It was a little unsettling at first to do without the things I so craved. So at the end of the first month I informally decided I would continue on with fasting for a few more weeks. It was a daily reminder of the sacrifice, a meal by meal acknowledgement of the price paid for me and a nightly denial of a food practice I've engaged in most of my adult life. My words might tend to make it sound bigger than it was. But in comparison to what Christ did for me it was all but nonexistent. But the practice, the act of considering what and how to fast, places the denial of oneself in the category of that of deliberate acts. With each successful act of discipline I was reminded that what I was doing was small in the scheme of things but it was still in the sight of God Himself. He was watching! He was cognizant of the act that I was engaging in, a physical practice of spiritual design and wellbeing.

So it was a successful fast. Even today I continue this fast occasionally in large part because it does remind me that He is with me, He is watching and He knows I love him even if in comparison it is a small thing. It is an outward show of a private practice of the one fasting by denying oneself that which is of value. As long as I kept my mind on why and for Whom I was fasting I was successful. Giving something up, something cherished, tends to refocus the spiritual life, too. It made me realize I can give things up, I can change things. That with His help I can make a difference in my life for Him.

And as you've read so far, my health is not the envy of the world. As a gastroenterologist once reminded me, "you are an enigma. Your kidneys are not trustworthy." I could be in a renal crisis with little or no warning and complete renal failure would likely result. I asked a specialist once why he took me on as a patient. "Well, even though I was not accepting new patients at the time, you were in a death spiral. I expected you would last no more than two months. So it would have likely been brief." That was nine years ago. So my kidneys are a problem. My present kidney disease stage is 3b, just a hop skip and a jump from stage 4, ending in renal failure shortly thereafter.

So just last week my blood was drawn for my regular quarterly tests. My results came in during the night and were quite astonishing, actually remarkable. My blood urea nitrogen test

(BUN) was 16, down from 24 just three months earlier, the lowest recorded for more than four years. The creatinine level was 1.70, the lowest in three and a half years and down from 1.98 just nine month ago. My glomerular filtration rate (GFR) was 41, up from 34 just a few months earlier and the best in years. And following those big improvements, my protein creatinine ratio was .6, also the best in four years. Now all these tests are measures of kidney sufficiency and might not mean much to you. But for someone like me that literally lives or dies by kidney function they are quite serious, serious improvement, unexpected improvement. The doctors have always maintained that due to the irreparable damage to my kidneys, age would only bring more irreversible deterioration. The best case would be continual slow deterioration until dialysis would be required. Well not in my case! These measures are much, much better. And I even lost sixteen pounds in the process, a much needed loss.

The first question by the rheumatology nurse practitioner was, "Tell me about this weight loss." She was concerned because I had received a positive test for cancer a few weeks earlier on a fecal examination. As we all know, unexplained weight loss is a symptom of many cancers and I might just have cancer. I will soon find out through endoscopic examination. I explained to her that the weight loss was intentional and if I have cancer, the weight loss is not a symptom. The weight is a symptom of fasting. My wife confirmed. The nurse practitioner actually charted it in her notes for the visit - "intentional weight loss through significant lifestyle changes and intermittent fasting". I'm saying I was rewarded openly - see below.

The spiritual endeavor, the practice of fasting, was under-appreciated and mostly misunderstood by this writer. But the act helped keep me focused on the cross, on the sacrifice, and ultimately made my appreciation of just what Jesus did for me to stay on the tip of my mind's tongue. I expect I will fast more often, for varying durations though not haphazardly, to stay in focus, keeping my eye on the cross and my faith in, and only in, the risen Savior.

And........I'm on a brief sabbatical from this fast tonight as I write. I resume again this coming Monday. It will be a regular part of my walk with Christ the rest of my life. Be careful what you read right on through. It might just improve your life both physically and spiritually. I have to say that I felt God's eyes on what I was doing. And that's a feeling I will routinely and actively seek. And as I close this chapter I am reminded what I wrote just a few paragraphs ago, you know, about making a connection with God. And that reassuring silent voice says to me that the connection with God was never lost, I just had to learn to recognize that which is always with me. I had to listen for it, mindfully aware that He is always with me. I am never alone, never alone indeed. And He sees.

I will fast. I will fast again.......and again..........

Moreover when ye fast, be not, as the hypocrites, of a sad countenance: for they disfigure their faces, that they may appear unto men to fast. Verily I say unto you, They have their reward.

But thou, when thou fastest, anoint thine head, and wash thy face;

That thou appear not unto men to fast, but unto thy Father which is in secret: and thy Father, which seeth in secret, shall reward thee openly.

Matthew 6:16-18 KJV

Chapter 14

The Total You

We were made in the image of God. That image was perverted early on in the history of God's creation. Paradise was lost and everlasting life had to come at a precious price, the most precious price ever paid for anything. The blood of the Son of God was spilled to wash us clean of our sins, availing to us the lost ability to live forever with God. The walk in the cool of the day with God was lost as well. So what replaced the walk in the cool of the day and why have I spoken of it so little in this work?

In the beginning Adam walked with God and I fully expect they talked face to Face. God abandoned the walks in the cool of the day. Sin was not something God could be in the presence of so walking in the cool of the day was over. Seeing God face to face was over. That kind of contact was lost. And I believe that was the true element that made paradise truly paradise, unhindered access to God. We still have that access but I believe we have turned it, almost and certainly in some cases, into a much abused privilege. And that access is truly a privilege.

In my first book "Will I Have Wings?" I devoted an entire chapter to our practice of prayer. In fact, it was the longest chapter in the book. I was quite critical of how we practice prayer in our daily lives and Christian walk. I will not, if at all possible, overemphasize it in this work. You can read it in the other book if you wish. To summarize our reaction, I believe we have turned it into a shopping list of just what we need God to do for us today. We have many asks as if God doesn't already know both our needs and our wants. If you do not know what I am referring to it's very likely you practice prayer quite differently than do most Christians. But for my purposes here I think the point I am trying to convey is just how critically vital prayer is to get to know God better. Mindfully catalyzing the heart for a growing and greater love of God comes from prayerful study. And in so doing, our soul, the essence of who we are, the part of us that goes to heaven can grow.

"And when thou prayest, Thou shalt not be as the hypocrites are: for they love to pray standing in the synagogues and in the corners of the streets, that they may be seen of men. Verily I say unto you, They have their reward. But thou, when thou prayest, enter into thy closet, and when thou hast shut thy door, pray to thy Father which is in secret; and thy Father which seeth in secret shall reward thee openly. But when ye pray, use not vain repetitions, as the heathen do: for they think that they shall be heard for their much speaking.   Be not ye therefore like unto them: for your Father knoweth what things ye have need of, before ye ask him."
Matthew 6:5-8 KJV

Are we going to enter through the gates of heaven with total surprise as to who God is? What a shame! The things I have associated with the almighty power of God in this book are just a small piece of the display of God's power. And to get to know God better, our study, our observations and our actions must be bathed in prayer with more of an ear for listening than with a mouth for begging. Wisdom! Why yes, ask for wisdom! Wisdom is available for the asking. As we gain in wisdom I would suggest that we will be far less frequent in asking for God to change His will to be more in line with what we think is the proper course of events here on earth. Our will is better than the will of God, no? Well of course it's not. But in our practice of prayer we sure come off like that sometimes.

"If any of you lack wisdom, let him ask of God, that giveth to all men liberally, and upbraideth not; and it shall be given him." James 1:5 KJV

We study everything in church these days, well, except we seldom if ever study the practice of prayer. Indeed, why should we study something so frequently practiced and taught in scripture by Jesus himself? Just why should we bother? It's because we slipped by Jesus' instructions on praying like we have done with so much of scripture. Jesus even gave us a prayer to go by. Do you know this prayer? Have you committed it to heart? Can you recall and recite it from memory? Is that ability even important? As a purely mechanical spiritual practice I suppose it is but does it provide that catalyst for the heart to grow in our relationship, our very personal connection with God? I will leave that for you to answer.

It's just me, but I'm not much for repeating myself to God at every event of praying. Though I do not fear praying in public, I do not spontaneously practice prayer on street corners. And, no, I see nothing wrong with it either. Jesus prayed in the presence of thousands. He also retreated to absolute privacy to pray for hours and hours. I just don't recall another instance in scripture where the time devoted to prayer by other people exceeded the private time devoted to the prayers of Jesus. He is the Model. Were those private prayers, the prayers in front of thousands and when He was teaching us to pray the limit of the prayer life of Jesus?

We make quite compelling arguments why we simply do not have time to devote hours to prayer. And hey, they are totally believable in today's hustle and bustle world. Who can retreat to the wilderness to pray for days and days when the bill collector is calling, the children are struggling in school or you are just plainly worn out? When the stock market is climbing and the lake is warm, when the beach is attracting our attention and money is plentiful, the time for a talk with God just flees us. But that argument fails when the market crashes, a tornado is in the front yard, a hurricane is in the gulf and we are flat broke. Suddenly, when threatened, we can just find all kinds of time to ask God to make it all go away. We are very much practicing prayer opportunely. Can you deny that? I certainly can't.

I would say that I think we are without blame in this busy world were it not for the times we go running to God to seek divine intervention to avoid a threat that might upset our apple cart. And I will paint with a broad brush here. I believe that we miss the part of prayer that is the very part that produces the soulful vitality that is available to us. That part of prayer is the spiritually cognizant, listening part of prayer. It's a large part of being always in prayer. Am I always in prayer? No I am not and I'm ashamed to admit it. I do, however, expect I'm in very good company. And many would admit it right along with me if they look in an honest, excuse free mirror. And while we are on the subject of being always in prayer I will admit another thing. I have been aware of the command to always be in prayer for years, in fact, most of my adult life. I just didn't give it the attention it deserved. I mean really, someone else will cover it in prayer, right?

Well, that's a big fat NO! Someone else might cover the same prayer request shared by a small group's class or the prayer for world peace. Even events very local to us like a weather threat, an earthquake or volcanic eruption might very likely, almost certainly be offered up to the Almighty with a request for protection from the elements. Even distant events that are small in the scheme of things globally but very personal to us like the crash of an airplane on which a friend or family member was a passenger might just be offered up by someone else. Someone else might even be quite local in their prayer for your health to be restored. But the big thing no one else can offer to your Lord is your personal, voiced, fervent praise of God the

Father, of God the Son and of the Holy Spirit. Nope, there is no one else that can cover your offering of prayer of praise and for personal worship time alone before God.

And just because someone else might voice a concern in prayer that you would ask doesn't mean a thing in your minute by minute walk with God. Just because the bases were covered so to speak doesn't mean you're playing ball. Your prayer might just be voiced in such a way that you draw nearer to God. I would not suggest that God learns anything about you. His omniscience demands that He knows even the least parts of your person. Considering His omniscience a little further, I try not to tell God things he obviously already knows. So how is it that we should carry on with our conversation with God if indeed He knows the entirety of our thoughts? It is certainly not because He needs our advice to make a decision. I am not intimating that prayer is a one way street, not at all. I am, however, suggesting that it is our time to display to ourselves in the view of God just what we're made of. And it is a time to receive much needed counseling from God.

The counseling that is available to us, I believe, is where always being in prayer is intended to be, the listening end of prayer, the cognizance that God is there. I believe we tend to overreact to things on the chance God needs to be made aware of an urgent matter. Is it conceivable that a child crossing a busy street unescorted is something we need to make urgently known to God? It sure is but it's not because God is unaware of the event or the potential danger to the child. Since the moment of creation, if not before, God had complete knowledge of the event. So why pray for protection of the child? Because it shows what our faith is all about. It shows we trust that God is able to protect the child. It shows that we turn to God when someone else is in distress. It shows God, and reflects in the mirror of our lives to us as well, a godly compassion for another of God's creations. Is it required that the prayer be noticeably dramatic for it to be heard by God?

Have you answered that question already? I will not question the motives of others but I would offer for your thoughts this: that a prayer made in public so quietly it's heard only by God is just as effective as a prayer made with the beat of a drum and a gymnastic display noticed by everyone. Have you ever offered a prayer just at the sound of the siren of an ambulance without even knowing who it is that occupies the back of the ambulance? Is it effective? I expect the effectiveness of a prayer is determined by the heart of the one offering the prayer. Is it prayer offered because we feel better about ourselves in so offering the prayer? Or is it a prayer offered that expresses a genuine concern for the one threatened, in the spirit of loving others even as we love ourselves? Praying is more about the relationship we have, the relationship we are allowing God to build in our lives.

Developing prayerfulness in our lives I believe to be a command not merely a suggestion. Obviously I must say, it is a lifelong battle to achieve in my life. But I continue to try. Answering myself, just what it is that I am, was important in this prayer life. I had to really cement in my mind that we are indeed God's creation. We are heart and mind joined prayerfully together into the soul that we will present ourselves into heaven as. The word and act "Prayerfully" cannot be overemphasized in our endeavor to spiritually enrich the soul into that which our hope will be to hear these words: "Well done, good and faithful servant!" I would submit that we are far too much talk and not nearly enough listening. I have tried to be a better listener, not just to listen more carefully to others, but to listen more carefully to what God has to say, to show me and to do in my life. It's hard, it truly is. There is so much competition for our attention, and at least for me, too much eagerness and willingness to respond before I have listened sufficiently and prayerfully sought the counsel of God. Very often I speak and act all too quickly before listening to the twenty four seven Counsel coming through to help me respond more like Him.

I am consoled to the fact that I will never be considered scholarly by others or in the mirror. That was not at all my purpose in life. I do believe I discovered what it is that God has for me in this, the earthly part of my everlasting life. And if it's visible that's alright with me. And if it is intended to be visible only to God I'm just as good with that. I am certain of many things far beyond dispute. I need more study of God's Word. I need to meditate more on what it is God is telling me. I need to hear more preaching on things I don't yet understand and on the things I feel I totally get too. And I need to develop as fully as I can that "always in prayer" state that we should all be in. I need to stay tuned in on what God has for me to hear and see. I believe it is far more important to hear what God has to say to me than what I might offer to Him as my thoughts on a matter. I need to deliver to God on that day He says "Come with Me", the soul He expects me to be, the real me. The soul He can say "Well done, good and faithful servant" to. I must admit, were I to be called at this instant, I fear God might mitigate that expression a good bit. Preparing to meet God face to Face, having a full and vibrant relationship with the Almighty requires being connected to Him by all those means afforded us. It is not just an unpracticed awareness of the spiritual arrows we have in our quiver, but the connection experience that comes from hitting the mark with them all, every time, all the time.

"His lord said unto him, Well done, good and faithful servant; thou hast been faithful over a few things, I will make thee ruler over many things: enter thou into the joy of thy lord."
Matthew 25:23 KJV

Prayer binds the heart and mind together to be the durable soul that will be the durable "you" that endures forever. And as I answered my son when he asked what he would be in heaven just a few weeks before he, in an instant, actually went to heaven, I said, "You will be you, son. You will be Alex and you will be Alex forever." It's what we are developing into while we fight the earthly battles. It's you. It's your soul. Yes, we will leave this body behind. And one day we will inhabit a new, incorruptible body and one day live on the New Earth, our forever home. It's heaven, right? You bet it is! Anywhere Jesus is indeed is heaven! And I am going! And I am going to do my prayerful best these last days of my life to present to God the best "me" I can be. It's only forever!

Engage that prayer life, that always in prayer mode of living while engaging in that walk in the cool of the day.....with Him. Nourish the soul with prayerful study, worship and praise with God right there with you.

"And I saw a new heaven and a new earth: for the first heaven and the first earth were passed away; and there was no more sea. And I John saw the holy city, new Jerusalem, coming down from God out of heaven, prepared as a bride adorned for her husband. And I heard a great voice out of heaven saying, Behold, the tabernacle of God is with men, and he will dwell with them, and they shall be his people, and God himself shall be with them, and be their God. And God shall wipe away all tears from their eyes; and there shall be no more death, neither sorrow, nor crying, neither shall there be any more pain: for the former things are passed away. And he that sat upon the throne said, Behold, I make all things new. And he said unto me, Write: for these words are true and faithful."
 Revelation 21:1-5 KJV

Chapter 15

A Walk in the Cool of the Day

Sometimes I think I would have liked to be Adam, the very first man. God walked with Adam in the cool of the day. Really, how would it feel to have a daily walk with the Creator of all that is, with the One that knows everything, your Maker. I at least envy Adam's walk with God in the cool of the day. I wonder if they talked about things while they walked. I expect they did. Adam had no one other than God himself to learn from. There were no experiences for Adam to draw from his terrestrial father and mother since he had neither. I believe they were both instructive and spiritually enriching walks, those walks in the cool of the day. Yes, I sure do wish I could have those walks in the cool of the day with God in the flesh. But that doesn't mean I can't walk with God in the cool of the day, or in the heat or freezing weather, in rain and wind and especially when I need Him most, when I am challenged by one thing or another.

I was never one much for walking in the cool of the day or any other time for that matter. And had I walked in the cool of the day for a large part of my life those walks would have been just a walk alone. Disease struck me and struck very hard nearly twenty years ago. I became so weak that even breathing sometimes took concentrated effort. It took a battery of doctors several years and multiple stabs at diagnoses to fully get the picture on just what was wrong with me. The initial onset of the disease lasted longer than the life expectancy for a Wegener's granulomatosis sufferer. But the treatment and partial relapse lasted about seven years. By the end of the treatment phase, first relapse and treatment again five years later I had all but given up. I really didn't care. I was fully ready to join my son in heaven.

As I began the slow recovery process to a stable new, compromised normal, an embattled immune system, and platelets that still haven't recovered, a hematologist suggested that I start walking. So walk I did, at first with assistance from my wife. And as I grew stronger, my walks became less of a labor and more of a walk in the cool of the day. Dread for my daily walk eventually morphed into longing as I progressed from a couple of hundred yards to two miles a day. It was physically therapeutic and that time became the starting point in my life when I was closest with God. It was my walk literally in the cool of the day, the part of the day with an emerging sunrise and a quiet time in the hood here in the hills of Tennessee. I was frankly struck by the awe of the never ever repeated sunrises. It seemed that God was painting them by hand just for me.

I really viewed the sunrise, I examined each and I still do, as my greeting straight from God. Walking in the silence of Windle Community, rarely disturbed by anything more than a snorting deer, I almost had to check beside me to make sure God wasn't walking with me in the nearly silent cool of the day. To say I'm an early riser would be a gross mischaracterization of my alarm clock free existence. The long term treatments for vasculitis had brought to my new reality what I thought were undesirable changes in my life. By the time the sun was just thinking about starting to rise, in the morning twilight, I would start my walk through the neighborhood. My breakfast was one cup of real coffee and two slices of dark toast with my own Armour and Pa's honey drizzled over it. So out I would go, water bottle in one hand and cell phone in the other.

The early morning and late evening are my favorite times of day. Those times bring the most widely varied colors to the middle Tennessee sky. It became a daily challenge to capture the beauty of the sunrise and post it on social media every single day. Have you ever thought an overcast day to be beautiful? If not, you've obviously just not been out enough to appreciate it. I thought the beauty of the sunrise colors in the skies of the east would eventually become commonplace. They did not. They became a thing that just made being thankful seem so appropriate. It was as if God painted them by hand just for me, just for David, for our joint enjoyment on our walk in the cool of the day. But as these walks in the cool of the day brought on more questions I just had to know more answers. Does God start with a new sky every morning or does today's beauty emanate from the point of creation. Is the sunrise just a consequence of His act of creation?

I will not opine on whether one or another sunrise was a personal gift from God to me because I have no way of knowing for sure. But that I find enjoyment in a particular sunrise or sunset was known to God before the sunrise was a sunrise. In fact, I believe that God, for lack of a better verb, programmed the natural events with full knowledge of them right from creation. I believe He knew then as He knew at that moment, and even now, that I would be seeing and appreciating his sunrise and viewing it as if He did it just for me. Omniscience is beyond my full comprehension, yet as I try to gain a better understanding of just what God knows, my full picture of God, my understanding of God grows.

My connection with the created natural world became really strong during my walks in the cool of the day. When the home just west of us was being built, well really during site preparation, large trees had to be removed. The logs from these trees were moved out to a clearing by which I walked. One morning very early as I was walking, a fully mature red fox was standing on top of one of the logs, my eyes connected with the fox's eyes. The fox neither feared me nor fled. It patiently but cautiously watched as I walked on by. I suspected that the fox's den had been disturbed by the clearing of the site where the house would soon stand. It was not an eerie feeling and I was not afraid of the fox. I read the fox as conveying the message to me that it knew what having one's life disturbed, changed forever meant. In a few minutes the fox disappeared into the woodland kind of hang dog like. I felt sorry for the fox. I wished there was something I could do to help the fox. Foxes, especially red foxes are so beautiful and pose no threat to humans. Just as quickly as the fox disappeared my walking companion in the cool of the day made me realize that He would, and does, see to the needs of the red fox just as He does mine.

My walks in the cool of the day continued well into winter. I missed very few days of walking in the cool of the day over several years. Occasionally I would move the time to the cool of the day around early afternoon because the normal cool of the day was below freezing. As I became stronger and my hemoglobin numbers reached normal levels I could concentrate on my walking companion more than my own safety. Where I live the speed limit is 45 miles per hour. Having a speed limit where I live is as meaningless as a "do not honk" sign in Midtown Manhattan. Several times I would catch myself all wrapped up enjoying my walk in the cool of the day when suddenly my walk would be interrupted with fleeing from death to one side of the road or the other. Loud exhaust pipes are popular here, some loud enough to hear for miles. But walking in the cool of the day with Him just makes the noise disappear. I wonder sometimes if He, invisible as He is, yanked me out of the danger of an oncoming car or truck.

In the cool of the day, when you let creation speak, you just hear the most wonderful sounds. Sometimes it speaks to the eyes. I suppose that is why I live where I live. No city is close by. A clear night's skyward view produces beautiful scenes of the created cosmos. Stars, the moon, occasionally some of the planets, and even other galaxies are presented away from the light polluted evenings of the cities. Many times, gazing away from the earth, I catch a momentary glimpse of a meteor entering our atmosphere and completely burning up in no more than an instant. Lately, with the aid of a camera and competent photographer we've witnessed the northern lights even this far south. Hey, in the middle of July and August the cool of the day here is often around midnight. The point being that He, God, is always available for that walk in the cool of the day.

The woodpeckers, owls, squirrels, bluebirds and yes, the snakes were sometimes along for the walk in the cool of the day. Over several years I began to understand the language in the Bible about even the rocks crying out. It seemed that every living thing acknowledged my walk in the cool of the day with my companion in visible absentia. No one ever heard me talking to God during my walk in the cool of the day but my words were meant for His ears only. Such questions as why are the brains in the woodpeckers not concussed from repetitive blunt force? Do they suffer from early onset dementia as did my mother? Why is the shape and set of the eye sockets of the owl so very different than those of the eagle? Why is the fox's tail so bushy? Why do pet dogs bark at me and the fox utters nary a whimper as I pass nearby? I never got those answers to a scientific conclusion because they really didn't matter. The answer I drew was this: That you appreciate My created world, that you observe it with Me in mind should answer your question. There are answers to all these questions but for the purpose of my walk in the cool of the day, the answer that quenched the wonder was that He did it. He did it and found it to be good. That works from me!

I have since abandoned most of my walking except for that necessary for property maintenance, caring for the honey bees and engaging with my grandson hunting or fishing. Plantar fasciitis has been a stone in my shoe for several months now, all but eliminating a physical walk in the cool of the day. Maybe, you think, He misses our walks in the cool of the Day? Is the stone in my shoe meant to put me back on the road again? It's possible I suppose but I'm really not avoiding my walk in the cool of the day. The walks in the cool of the day helped me hone my ability to walk with God just about all the time, even when someone else is with me. I talk a lot. My wife would argue quite successfully, that I very often talk too much. In the last third of my life I've tried to rein in the talking. I've had more than just a little success with it. And so it is that I have learned that my cool of the day walking companion is with me then too.

Just a couple evenings ago my daughter stopped by to deliver Valentine's Day candy to me and my wife. It might not have been candy that she gave Denise. I was more concerned with the candy she brought me. I have been on an after Christmas diet for six weeks but the candy is always welcome. I said, "Don't run off. Sit down and talk to us a little while." And so she did. We see far too little of our daughter though she lives just next door. She's immersed in the child rearing and working out of the home years of her life. She's a good mother and an excellent eye doctor. She beats them both as a daughter. And so I caught myself listening to the events of her week, rarely saying anything in return. And sure enough, it was a walking in the cool of the day moment. I thought as she talked to us, what a wonderful piece of creation God gave me. To listen to her for nearly an hour was such a treat. I see a little of me, a lot of her mother, and even more of God's influence in her life, a rewarding walk in the cool of the day, continuously seated I might add. I am so proud of her and the display of Christ in her life. It is a gift I believe, to walk with God in the cool of the day even though it is not just the same way as did Adam.

And then I wonder, what if I had been Adam? Would I have fallen from Grace too? With all I have available to me would I have still fallen? Adam had no Bible, not so much as a laptop or tablet. He had no preacher to set him on the straight and narrow. For a while Adam didn't even have a companion. He was alone in all of creation. No television and certainly no televangelists. Did he tithe and just where did this tithe go?

There were no banks, no church houses, no parsonage, no police station, no national organizations and no charities for Adam to be concerned with. His phone didn't ring off the hook from telemarketers and robocalls. He had no decision about when to retire and whether or not to have traditional Medicare or an Advantage plan. He had no external guidance, no Sunday School teacher and no one had yet written a book. Adam just had Adam and the entirety of the created world, the world created by his walking companion in the cool of the day, God himself.

What sadness must have fallen on Adam when the physical walk with God in the cool of the day came to an end! I wonder, had he learned to walk with God in the cool of the day without God there with him? Did he rebel? I wonder just how old Adam was when this change occurred. I never had God walk with me face to Face, in the flesh so to speak. I expect Adam never conceived of losing the privilege of walking in the cool of the day with God. To say that the disobedience of Adam and Eve was devastating is the understatement of this book, maybe of all time. Adam knew He was walking with God. Adam knew of God's absence from the walk in the cool of the day. I just have to believe that Adam was absolutely crushed by the loss of such a close relationship with God. He never knew death, hardship or abandon until He lost his walking Companion. Paradise was lost indeed in the world of Adam. I don't believe that walk in the cool of the day was ever exactly replicated after the fall.

Actually, I believe, really I know, that God walked with others. But this time God presented himself to the world as the Son of a woman, a virgin, and the very Son of God. Jesus walked on the face of the earth with many. I wonder just when they realized they were walking with God incarnate, the Messiah. They had been waiting for His appearance for thousands of years and when He came He came as an infant. Jesus walked with many people during his life. And these people walked Him to His death on a cross. Soldiers mocked and spat on him. He was struck on the face, flogged to within an inch of HIs life. He was beaten so very severely that I expect His own mother had trouble recognizing Him. And He was killed on the cross.

He was without guilt. I have heard some say that if He was truly God incarnate that He gravely miscalculated by returning to earth as He did just to let His own creation have its way with Him, even to His death. I beg to differ. Jesus knew exactly what He was doing. He knew it from even the point of creation. You just cannot be truly omniscient and miss a few key things, even those of triviality. Jesus' return was a calculated return, a return that He was singularly capable of, a return that would present the world with a sacrifice truly and absolutely without blemish, the only sacrifice sufficient to save the world, even Adam. Have I written that a few times herein? Do you get it? And even me, He paid the price to redeem me!

And so what have I drawn from my walks in the cool of the day, walking with God physically in absentia? No, I have not concluded that the creation is God. Nor have I concluded that the creation created God. And I see no evidence that anything but multiple gods would have followed the desires of men to have a god, more to the point, gods. But these gods would be created by man and not the Creator of all that is. But I do see evidence, irrefutable evidence that God, in the flesh, did walk here in the cool of the day with Adam. I have concluded that Jesus walked with many here in the flesh. I am convinced to a certainty that Jesus is indeed the Son of almighty God and that He walks with me in the cool of the day......and when I am studying His Word, and when I go fishing and when I am with my grandson and listening to my daughter and driving and working in the garden and marveling in the work of a beekeeper. Yes, it seems my walks with Him just get more involved in my life as I approach the end of the usefulness of this body.

The Spirit of God walks with me all the time. I do look for Him in my walk through life. And most often I recognize Him in the things that He made. He is just visible everywhere. Ashamedly, I admit that sometimes I ignore His presence. But then He nudges me back into acknowledging His presence in my life, in my walk in the cool of the day, with Him. Walking in the cool of the day with God is a most precious experience. There is just no other way to walk through life than walking with Him in the cool of the day, walking with Him all the time. He is the Way! He is the only Way. Start that walk! Walk with God! He stands and knocks……the opportunity to walk in the cool of the day with God is still available. Draw near to him and He will draw near to you. The cool of the day, well really, is all the time!

"Behold, I stand at the door and knock: if any man hear my voice, and open the door, I will come in to him, and will sup with him, and him with me." Revelation 3:30 KJV

About the Author

David E. Wright, author of "Will I Have Wings?" attended high school at Alvin C. York Agricultural Institute in Jamestown, Tennessee, his home until going to college. He graduated from Tennessee Technological University in 1980 with a degree in Economics and Finance. He and his wife, Denise, have been married forty five years. His daughter, Dr. Ashley Wright Allred, is an optometrist and her husband, Andy, teaches elementary school mathematics. David chose business as his career in life and worked in administration in companies engaged in oil and gas exploration, commercial fixtures manufacturing, textiles, defense contracting, metal fabrication and team sports apparel and equipment. After school he started his first job as a roughneck on an oil drilling rig, moving into administration in just a few days. He left the business and financial world in 2014 after being diagnosed with a rare form of vasculitis. He worked for thirty five years with duties ranging from office management to President and Chief Executive Officer of a national company. He is a full time grandpa, his true calling, residing in Livingston, Tennessee for the past forty five years, presently living next door to his beloved daughter Ashley, her husband Andy and their son Armour. He enjoys hunting and fishing, beekeeping, gardening, playing the banjo, traveling and developing his relationship with God ………and being Pa.

Made in the USA
Columbia, SC
16 June 2025

59270061R00087